CARING
FOR
YOUR

CAT

CARING
FOR
YOUR

CAT

Howard Loxton

BLACK CAT

First published in 1985
by Macdonald & Co. (Publishers) Ltd
as *The Cat Repair Handbook*
Reprinted in 1989 by Macdonald & Co.
(Publishers) Ltd
under the Black Cat imprint

Text © Howard Loxton 1985, 1989
Cartoons © Gray Jolliffe 1985, 1989

ISBN 0-7481-0255-8

Macdonald & Co. (Publishers) Ltd
66-73 Shoe Lane
London EC4P 4AP

A member of Maxwell Pergamon Publishing
Corporation PLC

Printed in Italy by New Interlitho

Contents

Introduction

There are three types of people who may be reading this book: those who are thinking of investing in a furry rodent-catcher because they have failed to find a mousetrap with a built-in homing device; those who believe themselves to be animal lovers and are contemplating adding a feline friend to their household; and those who, having previously been the second, now find themselves sharing their lives with a creature that wrecks their home and plays havoc with their self-control as they bandage their lacerated hands and plug their ears to its howls.

If you are the first type, be warned that no cat comes with a guarantee (despite old Welsh and Saxon laws that rated cats by their ability to catch mice), and some show no interest at all in catching them – and may even decide to adopt a family of mice as their own pets! If you do not pride yourself on being an animal lover – and obviously you do not, or why persecute the poor mice anyway – then get in the local 'rodent operative' to deal with them and avoid the responsibilities that cat ownership entails.

If you *do* love animals, how far does your tolerance go? Read on and take heed of the advice that follows if you do not want to risk removal in a straitjacket. Of course, some cats are perfect and well-behaved and you could be lucky, but . . .

Cats are independent beings and, in historical terms, have been domesticated comparatively recently, only three thousand years or so ago, whereas dogs have been domesticated since man's earliest hunting days. Just look at the variety of different shapes and sizes of dogs, all with different aptitudes – there is the evidence of their long domestication, while cats are all much more alike and obviously closer to their wild origins. Dogs are pack animals that instinctively follow a leader and so they can easily be trained. Cats are not; they are independent animals and do not take kindly to being given orders. However, they are domestic animals and have become dependent upon people to provide some, if not all, their needs.

The housecat depends upon man entirely, and cat ownership is a responsibility not lightly to be undertaken. Food, shelter, health, safety and even the sex life of the cat all come under your control. Just being an animal lover is not enough to warrant your certification as suitable for cat ownership. Can you offer the cat a good home and proper care? You can keep a cat without passing a government inspection or qualifying for a special licence, of course, but it is just as well to see if you can pass the Cat Ownership Test (COT).

Try the COT. Answer the following questions:

1. **Do you**
   a) keep regular hours, or
   b) go out on the razzle several times a week?
2. **Are you**
   a) a stay-at-home, or
   b) often away at weekends or for holidays?
3. **Are you**
   a) the tolerant, laid-back type, or
   b) easily annoyed?

4. **Is your house**
   a) well away from traffic, or
   b) in a city or by a busy road?
5. **Do you**
   a) have plenty of spare time, or
   b) lead a very busy life?
6. **Are**
   a) possessions of little importance to you, or
   b) do you pride yourself on the good things in your home?
7. **Do you**
   a) know how much it costs to feed a cat, or
   b) are you so rich that it does not matter?
8. **Do you**
   a) 'rise and shine' at the same time every morning, or
   b) lie around in bed for as long as possible at weekends?
9. **Do you**
   a) know what vets charge for consultations, or
   b) believe animals should deal with their own illnesses?
10. **Do you**
   a) regularly take snuff, or
   b) suffer from hay-fever or other allergies?

Are you a suitable cat owner?

How did you do in the COT? If you answered 'a' to everything, then a cat may find your home very suitable – though you might find yourself being owned by the cat, rather than the other way around. A few 'b's will not rule you out (especially if one of them was to Question 7, provided that does not mean that you are just plain irresponsible), but you should put off getting a cat until you have read every chapter of this book and thought carefully about what will be involved.

Now let's take a look at the points that the COT highlights.

1. Cats tend to be creatures of habit. They like their meals on time and to know exactly when they can expect to be let in or out – if they cannot get you to dance attendance on them all the time. They must learn to tolerate occasional changes in routine, but too much disruption could result in a troublesome pet. Like most animals, cats are natural conservatives.

2. Who will look after a cat if you are not there? Can you really rely on friends or neighbours to come in to maintain the cat's routine? For holidays you can try boarding at a cattery (though it will not suit every cat, and you may have to book well ahead), but taking it there and collecting it will take up time, and there will be fees to pay.

3. An occasional irritating mishap is inevitable and probably cannot be blamed on the cat, while demands for attention at the wrong time can seem like pestering. There is no use chastising a cat for a misdemeanour unless you catch it in the act, for the cat will associate your displeasure with what it is doing at the time rather than what it did wrong earlier. This can lead to some very unfortunate consequences.

4. Traffic is always a hazard. Some cats learn to do their kerb-drill before streaking to the other side, but many people do not think that their cat should take a chance and instead keep it indoors. That is not to suggest the countryside is safe, either – kittens can end up as a meal for a marauding fox, and cats not used to traffic will be less wary of a vehicle.

5. Buying and preparing food, changing litter, grooming and the occasional visit to the vet can eat up a lot of time – and your cat will expect you to find time to play with it. These 'few minutes' all add up, especially when you are late for work.

6. A cat's claws can do irreparable damage to curtains, carpets and furniture, and a snag in your favourite skirt or trousers can relegate them to second-best. Of course you can train a cat – but even then it may persist in inflicting deliberate damage in an attempt to get its own way. No cat, and especially no kitten, can be blamed for the occasional incontinence due to excitement or fear (or to being locked in without a tray, or to over-soiled litter), and if sick it may vomit on your Persian carpet. Have you ever tried to get rid of the smell of cat's pee? (See page 32.) If you have valuable furniture and rugs, or a house full of precious ornaments, are you prepared to put them at risk?

7. You do not have to feed a cat on Scotch smoked salmon to run up bills. You are committing yourself to a can of food a day, 365 days a year – and cats live to over fifteen years. Take a look at current pet food prices – and fresh meat may cost much more! Would you not rather spend the money on a trip around the world?

8. Cats do not always learn that Sunday is different – and even when they know it perfectly well, may still be determined to wake you up and threaten to wreck the place if you do not get breakfast to them at once.

9. Even if your cat is *never* sick, some vet's fees (for neutering and vaccinations, for example) cannot be avoided, unless you can find an animal welfare clinic to provide them for free. Serious medical problems can lead to big bills. Can you afford them? You also have to find time to take the cat to the vet and to be its nurse at home.

10. Some people get a sneezing fit the moment they go into a house that has a cat. Fine fibres of fur in the air or on furnishings are usually the cause. Regular grooming and frequent vacuum-cleaning of furniture and carpets will reduce the problem – and some breeds shed less fur than others – but all cats moult, so check on you and your household's allergic reactions before you get a cat. Otherwise you may discover too late that the price of feline companionship is a frequent dose of antihistamine.

What you really have to consider are your personal priorities – and if you have not already been put off the whole idea of cat ownership, you probably qualify under the COT and can surmount any difficulties that may arise. Only a few cats are monsters – though every one can be as devious as the devil – and a contented cat can be the most rewarding and affectionate of pets.

The rest of this book will help you to anticipate feline problems and guide you in dealing with them. By increasing your knowledge of cats, and of their behaviour, you will equip yourself to be a better owner. Soon you will wonder how you ever managed to conceive of life without a cat, and agree with Mark Twain that 'a home without a cat, and a well-fed, well-petted and properly revered cat, may be a perfect home, *perhaps*, but how can it prove its title?'

Buying a cat for others

Do not! Or at least, not without making sure that the cat is wanted and that the recipient is capable of looking after it properly. Having a cat is often thought to help a child learn responsibility, but an irresponsible child will almost certainly result in an unhappy and badly behaved cat, and both will have to be cared for by the parents.

Make sure the recipient can afford both time and money to feed and care for a pet. Too many kittens are given for birthdays or as Christmas presents, or bought when the summer holidays begin and children are at home, only to be taken to a vet a few months later to be put down or, worse still, abandoned to struggle on their own.

1. Taking the plunge

Having thought it over seriously and decided that you really want to get a cat, what kind should it be?

All cats may be grey in the dark, but over the past century many different breeds have been developed. They do not display the great physical differences that distinguish the types of dog, most of which have been bred over hundreds, or even thousands, of years to perform particular tasks. Cats have been bred for appearance, not for work. However, the three main groups – Longhairs, Shorthairs and Orientals (or Foreign Shorthairs as they are officially known in Britain) – do have more than just aesthetic differences.

Long-haired cats are often quieter and more placid than the others, so if you want a cat that will sit quietly on a cushion waiting to be stroked and admired, a Longhair (or Persian, as they used to be called, and still are, in America) would be a good choice. The snag is that their long, silky fur requires a lot of grooming – a job for you the owner, for the glamorous coat is more than they can cope with on their own.

Like Longhairs, Domestic Shorthairs may also curl up for hours and snooze – all cats spend a lot of time asleep – but they tend to be more animated and their coat is much easier to keep in trim.

Orientals, and especially the Siamese, will certainly remind you of their presence. They are much more people-centred than Longhairs or Shorthairs, and like to be involved in everything that is going on. They make excellent companions, if that is what you want, for they demand attention, but they often do so with a very penetrating voice, which some people find irritating. Because they are usually more attached to people than to places, they are more likely to adjust to frequent changes of location than a cat that becomes very attached to its territory – useful if your life-style means you have to move frequently.

There are a whole range of pedigree cat breeds in all three groups (see pages 121–130 for more details), and mongrels too will fall broadly into one type or another.

that you can be sure what a kitten will look like when full grown and what its offspring will look like, which is important to take into account if aesthetic considerations play a large part in your choice. Some breeds also have distinctive traits of character. However, a cat's personality will probably owe as much to its immediate ancestry – the personality of its parents – and its rearing as to breed type. Breeders will obviously favour breeding from cats with personalities that they like, so inspecting other cats in a cattery can be a guide.

A visit to a cat show will enable you to see a large number of breeds at once and give you the chance to talk to exhibitors. You may also be able to discover the names of breeders and the addresses of cat organizations, often given in the show catalogue. Owners are usually delighted to talk about their cats and their characteristics; you will have more trouble stopping them than getting them started.

Pedigree cats will cost more than moggies, but mongrels can be as attractive, have just as much character as a thoroughbred, and be just as intelligent (or stupid). You may only be able to guess at their paternity, but if you know their mother's personality you can expect that some of her temperament and conditioning will be passed on.

Moggie or pedigree?

So which do you go for: a moggie or a pedigree? Pedigree cats will conform fairly closely to the 'standard', the official description, for their breed. This means

Cat or kitten?

Acquiring a young kitten will give you the chance to train it in the way you want

someone who finds it difficult to get about, or if no one is at home during the day to provide the frequent meals and attention that young kittens need.

Male or female?

If you have decided on a kitten, then, unless you intend to breed, its sex is not of great importance because it is advisable to have it neutered when it reaches an appropriate age (see page 78). If you *do* want to breed, it is easier to have a female and to take her to a stud male for mating if she is a pedigree (though females will usually have no difficulty finding a tom for themselves if allowed outside in season). Stud cats do not really make household pets because they require special housing and care.

To the uninitiated the sexual organs of young male and female kittens do not look very different, but an experienced breeder is not likely to make an error in sexing. As a rough guide, the male rear presents two small circles, like a colon (:), and the female a dotted 'i'. The difference is easier to see when you can view the two sexes together.

Finding a cat

There are many sources for a cat or kitten – pet stores, breeders, animal welfare organizations, friends and neighbours – or a stray cat may size up the prospects of your home, like the look of them, and

and to affect its behaviour by the security and confidence you can give it. However, do not necessarily choose a kitten. There are many grown cats in need of a new home because their owners can no longer look after them, or that have been abandoned and taken to animal refuges. It is very rewarding to gain the confidence of a cat that has come to distrust people because of earlier ill treatment. If you take on an adult cat from someone you know, then you will know something of its personality and how it has been trained and you should have no unexpected problems. All adult cats may require a little more adjustment to a new home than a kitten, but it is not just the older cat that you will be doing a favour. Captivating though a kitten may be, an older cat is likely to be less prankish and is less likely to rush around causing accidents and getting under your feet. It may be a better choice for a senior citizen or make the choice for you. Unless you actually want to give a stray a home, find it another or pass it on to an animal welfare organization as soon as possible or you will land yourself with a new and permanent companion. Similarly, do not be pressured into taking a cat or kitten from a neighbour. However, giving a home to a cat in need will at least save it from joining the thousands that welfare organizations have to put to sleep each year, as will taking one from a cat refuge.

If you do take in a stray, a check-up at the vet would be a sensible precaution, and you should certainly look out for signs of fleas, worms or mites. You should also try to trace the cat's owner before considering it to be yours. A stray or a cat from a welfare refuge may feel insecure and untrusting if it has been badly treated in the past, and require more careful handling than one from a secure home. You should watch out for any vices or bad behaviour traits that have developed and require retraining. Stealing socks, like some feline fetishists, may not be much of a hazard, but peeing in every corner could cause you problems.

Pet stores are the obvious place to look for a kitten, but their standards often leave a lot to be desired. Ill or unhappy

looking animals, or untidy surroundings, should be avoided at all costs. And be firm: do not lose your heart to some little kitten because it looks sick and sad, needing just *your* care. You will almost certainly let yourself in for endless trouble, mounting vet bills and eventual heartbreak if the kitten cannot be restored to health. There are always plenty of healthy kittens needing homes.

Unless a breeder does not want to be bothered with selling to the public, or the cattery is very remote – in which case he or she may prefer to deal through a store – most of his or her kittens are likely to be sold direct, so you are less likely to get show-quality cats through a pet store. If you want a pedigree cat but do not know a cattery that breeds the type you want, your local vet may be able to put you in touch with one, or the breed society supply a list of breeders, while show catalogues often carry advertisements.

When you have tracked down a breeder, do not expect to obtain a kitten straight away. Sometimes the popularity of a breed outstrips the availability of kittens and they are booked well ahead. In any case, your first visit to a breeder is the time to take a look at the cattery, to see how well run it is and judge the health of the cats. Ask to look at all the cattery 'queens' – the technical name for breeding females – and discuss their characteristics and personalities with the owner.

If you are not interested in breeding or showing but simply want a pet, then make this clear at the start. Some breeders prefer their 'best' kittens – those with the most perfect shape, colour, and markings for the show bench – to go only to people who intend to breed from them. Delightful kittens that do not match those criteria (and that you might even find more attractive) will probably be less expensive.

Even if you find an available kitten, you may not be able to take it there and then, for no kitten should leave its mother until it is at least six, and preferably more than eight, weeks old. In any case, unless you have already made provision at home for the kitten's arrival, it would be very unwise to take it straight away. No good breeder will press a kitten upon you. He will be as eager to check that you are going to be a suitable cat owner as you are to obtain a kitten. Few cat breeders are out to make a fortune; they just love cats.

If no kittens are currently available, you can always ask to reserve one from a future litter. Arrange to see the litter when as young as possible, and if the cattery is near your home, make several visits to watch the development of the kittens and choose the one that is right for you.

Choosing a kitten

Wherever you go to find a kitten, you obviously want to choose a healthy one, so look out for any tell-tale signs of illness or infestation – not only in your selected kitten, but in any other cats in the cattery or pet store.

If you are allowed to handle a kitten – and you should be, provided you have not been in contact with other cats from which you might pass on disease – you should not feel any hard or scabby patches of skin under the fur. The fur itself should be free of any powdery deposit, which might suggest a skin condition, and of the black specks that could be the droppings of fleas. The eyes should be bright and follow everything with interest. Neither they nor the nose should have any runny discharge, and the ears should be clean and free from gummy fluid or brown specks that result from ear mites (see page 108).

At the other end, look for any signs of diarrhoea or the rice-grain-like segments around the anus that indicate tapeworm. The belly should feel rubbery, not hard or flabby, while a blown-out stomach is a sign of worms.

Does it lean too much to one side or keep shaking its head (ear problems again), or scratch itself incessantly (flea infestation)? How does the kitten move? Has it a strong action, or do its legs look weak? Does it play with its siblings and hold its own, or does it cower timidly in a corner? Beware of the smallest and shyest of the litter, probably the runt; it is unlikely to be as robust as the others. Pick a kitten that is playful and inquisitive, although not necessarily the boldest – the dominant kitten may prove to be the most difficult to discipline. Boss cats will try to boss you, too – and the evidence suggests they usually succeed! Of course, you may lose your heart to one particular kitten and so will probably ignore all this wise advice – but at least you cannot say you were not warned that only healthy kittens should be chosen.

Taking possession

When you come to take charge of a new cat or kitten, make sure the previous owner sorts out all the appropriate documents and briefs you on the diet and routine to which the cat is accustomed. If you are not actually given a diet sheet, then make a note of what, when and how much you should feed the new arrival. Find out whether it has been wormed, and whether it has had any vaccinations against cat diseases. Immunized cats should have vaccination certificates that will indicate the type of vaccine and when the next injections should be given.

A pedigree cat should be accompanied by a pedigree certificate. For showing or breeding, a pedigree cat must be registered with the appropriate body, and its ownership formally transferred to you. Ask the breeder to do this or to give you the appropriate forms and to explain what to do.

This is also the time to raise any queries with the breeder or owner. It is much easier to settle things face to face than to telephone for help later, or to follow instructions in this or any book. If this is your first cat, then ask to be shown how to do any of the things described later in this book that may be new to you.

Holding a cat

Even such an apparently simple thing as how to hold a cat is not so obvious, and many people do it wrongly. For example, you probably know that mother cats carry their kittens by the scruff of the neck, holding them with their teeth.

With a young kitten that is an acceptable way of picking it up (though you should use your fingers, not your teeth), but put your other hand beneath the kitten to support its body as soon as you have lifted it off the ground. It is not a good way to pick up, let alone carry, an older cat, though it is a good hold to exert restraint or to grab a panicking one.

The proper way to lift a grown cat is by putting one hand beneath its body and lifting behind the forelegs, while cupping the other hand beneath its rump as you lift it from the floor. A tiny kitten can be cradled on the palm of your hand, perhaps with your fingers lifted under the neck to support its head, but most cats should be carried on the crook of your arm or held against your body. With both arms in front of your body you can support a cat's main weight on one forearm, its front paws on the other, leaving that

hand on the outside to stop the cat slipping or jumping down. But the main thing is to find a position comfortable for you and the cat. The crucial thing is to support all of its weight, not just to let it straddle your arm. Some cats – perhaps the more inquisitive kind – like to sit on your forearm, leaning against your body with their paws over your shoulder. The exact position will vary according to cat and owner, but both must be comfortable. A cat's weight must be supported and it must be held firmly enough not to be able to jump away – but at the same time not squeezed so that it feels trapped.

Most cats do not much like being cradled on their backs as you would carry a baby – though there are exceptions that are very gentle and prefer it, especially if their tummy is tickled! However, do not take risks; in this position a cat could reach up at your face and scratch you very badly.

Before you go

Other things you should take the opportunity to be shown are how to give a pill and how to deal with grooming, clawtrimming and other routine procedures.

Make sure you have the owner or breeder's address and telephone number before you leave, and not just in case you need more information or advice. After having bred and reared a cat, most breeders will be interested in its future progress. I know one who goes so far as to give a number of stamped and addressed postcards to purchasers of kittens to ensure she gets reports on their progress for the first few months.

When the cat or kitten is in its travelling basket and you are ready to leave, do not forget to check the fastenings on the basket – you do not want an escape halfway to home. Take all the cat's documentation with you, which will form the nucleus of a file that should eventually include any pedigree and registration forms, vaccination certificates and medical records (including reactions to treatment), dates of season for an unneutered female, addresses and telephone numbers of breeder, vet and boarding catteries, and a photograph of your cat, which will help if you have to describe it, should it ever get lost. You will be surprised how difficult it can be to answer even a simple question, such as your cat's age, if you do not have a record of it.

Now you are ready to take your new charge home – but is your home ready for it? The preparations you should make before going to pick up your new pet are described in the next chapter.

2. Preparing for pussy

Sometimes a cat or kitten will take one look at a new home, decide that it is just what it was looking for and curl up on the nearest lap. More often it will first need to recover from the trauma of being shoved in a basket and taken on a journey (probably for the first time in its life) without any idea of what is going on, then finding itself in a strange place surrounded by people it has never met before and even being intimidated by large barking creatures with furiously wagging tails. Imagine it happening to you.

It requires strategy and careful planning to ensure that the installation of a new arrival in the home goes smoothly – for you as well as the cat. There are decisions to be made and equipment to be bought before the red-letter day when the newcomer actually arrives. If you want to strike up the right relationship with your cat from the start then you must ensure that it has all it needs to adapt comfortably to your household.

Equipment

Let's take equipment first. At one time cats and dogs just ate off the floor and slept in a shed but now a whole industry produces special pet paraphernalia. You should obtain:

Travelling baskets

Carrying a cat or kitten in your arms is far too risky, especially if this is the first time it has gone out into the world. A sudden fright (let us hope not the mere sight of you) could make it leap out of your arms and bolt for cover – straight under the nearest bus or up a fire escape. Even in a car a kitten could easily cause confusion or worse by startling the driver or obstructing the pedals – and then you may face the unpleasant choice of a crumpled car or a crumpled cat.

Traditional carrying baskets are made of wicker, but lightweight fibreglass and plastic-covered wire are easier materials to clean and disinfect. For very short-term use, ventilated cardboard boxes with carrying handles are often available from vets and pet stores, but they are not very durable and a determined cat may claw and bite its way out, given time or a box weakened from use. They are valuable in emergencies but it is well worth investing in a permanent carrier. Some more expensive models are fitted with comfortable bedding and built-in water bowls, but whatever type you choose, the things to check are the fastenings, which must be secure and not openable by a stray paw. Many baskets open at the side but it is easier to lift a cat out of an opening at the top.

Food and water bowls

Ordinary dishes or saucers can be used to feed your cat but they can be easily spilled by the pressure of a paw on the side and, as a hygienic precaution, you have to remember to keep them separate from similar dishes used for the family. Pottery or plastic bowls, shaped so that they do not spill, are much better and cheaply available. There are also sophisticated food dispensers on the market including one type which works like a pedal bin: by stepping on a flat panel in front of the dish, the cover is raised. A cat soon learns to use one, though if it tends to wolf down all its food the moment it is served the clever cover is hardly necessary! The more complicated the apparatus the more expensive and difficult to keep clean – but worth investigation if your cat does not insist on dragging food out of its bowl.

Litter trays

This is the cat's lavatory. When kittens are small, you could use an old oven tray, providing its roasting days are over, but a tough plastic tray from a pet store is cheap and easy to clean. For kittens the sides should not be higher than 3 in (7.5 cm) so that they can climb over comfortably. In it you put a layer of earth, sand, peat or commercial litter (usually prepared from fuller's earth or some other absorbent clay) which is not cheap but is more hygienic.

Some trays have detachable rims which can be used to secure a disposable plastic liner and help to reduce the amount of litter scattered outside. Others have a dome-like cover which will not only keep the litter in but also help to contain any smell not neutralized by a commercial litter formula. Whether your cat will prefer an opaque cover to give it privacy or a transparent one to avoid claustrophobia is something you will have to guess – unless you can arrange with a pet store to take one on (the cat's) approval. There are even trays on the market designed for reusable litter. They are expensive but can be economical in the long run if you and the cat find them acceptable.

Economy tips
Use a scoop to remove solids and lumps from the litter to make it last longer. Line the tray with a wad of newspaper to absorb moisture. A thin scattering of litter, frequently changed, will use less than a deep layer changed less often.

Beds

A cat needs somewhere to sleep that it can call its own. It may *prefer* to sleep somewhere quite different, for example on your bed or on the central heating boiler (and more about that later), but its own base will help to satisfy its territorial needs. All kinds of cat beds are now available from the threadbare to the downright extravagant: conventional wicker baskets, formed fibreglass shapes, bean-bag nests, housing with built-in heating units and arrays of poles to climb, fully covered sleeping shelters and feline adventure playgrounds – but most cats seem to love an ordinary cardboard box which they can jump in and out of at will, with several layers of newspaper as lining and an old blanket on the top that they can curl up on or even snuggle under. These you can throw away when they get dirty and replace at little cost.

If your tastes (and pocket) run to a more sophisticated arrangement, pet stores will be delighted to encourage you, your home may look a little tidier and, since all felines are sybaritic creatures, your cat may approve of any added luxury you can give it but still go back to its cardboard box! Cats place their own idea of comfort before any aesthetic considerations or current fashion.

But be warned: if you do pamper your pet *never* use an ordinary domestic electric blanket in its bed – folding them can interfere with their safety and they are not claw- and waterproof. Use only heating units made specially for pet use, and follow safety instructions.

Collars and leads

Even if you have no plans to take your cat out for walks a collar and lead will be useful as a means of control and restraint when you have to take it to the vet or on a journey. The collar must have an elastic section, so that if the cat gets caught on a nail or twig it can free itself without risk of choking. The collar should also carry an identity disc with the address and/or telephone number of its owner, or a cylinder that holds a roll of paper on which they can be written. The cylinder type is useful if you move around a lot and have to keep on changing your address, but the disc will be more easily noticed and read.

For those who intend to walk their cat on a lead a harness is better than a collar, but it is difficult to find one to fit a small kitten and a collar will anyway be needed if the cat is to be allowed out on its own.

Scratching-posts or panels

These can be a piece of log, or carpeting or coarse fabric such as hessian mounted on a post or panel on which the cat can exercise its claws – rather than on your furniture or furnishings. It is absolutely essential to provide a post or panel for a cat kept entirely indoors, though you could substitute an old piece of furniture if you do not mind having a chair torn to shreds! Both panels and posts can be obtained ready-made from a store.

Kitten comforts

If your new acquisition is a kitten leaving mother and siblings for the first time, get a clock with a loud tick – an old-style wind-up clock is just the thing. The idea is not to wake the kitten up – at that age it should be allowed to sleep as much as it likes – but to provide a substitute for its missing family (see pages 27–8 for what you should actually do with the clock). Unless you have splashed out on the luxury of a heating panel for the bed then a hot-water bottle (thick rubber, metal or ceramic) is another thoughtful extra to have ready.

Toys

Kitten or cat, your new pet should have some playthings. Pet stores stock all kinds of toys from simple stuffed mice and pipe-cleaner spiders to balls mounted on springs or elastic and mice that pop in and out of holes like the figures on a cuckoo clock. No doubt in the more expensive emporia for the pampered pussy you could even buy radio-controlled rodents and other space-age gadgets. However, a crumpled ball of paper, a cotton reel, a table-tennis ball, a cardboard box big enough to get inside and a sheet of newspaper, placed tent-like with the fold as the ridge so that it can be dashed beneath, will all give hours of fun.

Shops often sell toy mice stuffed with catnip, a plant that cats usually like, and these are better than toys stuffed with materials that might do harm if eaten. If a toy has eyes make sure that they are secure and do not buy anything on which toxic paints or dyes have been used. Like small children, young cats will instantly demolish most playthings, so get the toughest ones you can find.

Preparations

Before you actually arrive home with your new cat, you should make some preliminary decisions about where you are going to let it go in the house and where you are going to feed it and put its bed and litter tray. Areas designated out of bounds should be firmly established as such from the start.

Food bowls need to be placed where you will not keep tripping over them (or the cat) and where spills can be contained

– some cats make a point of dragging their food out of the bowl! For protection, place the bowls – one for food, one for water and one for milk – on a newspaper or plastic sheet to keep the surface below clean. The litter tray you will probably want to put relatively out of sight, but it should be easy for the cat to get to and accessible for changing. For the cat's bed, find a quiet place that is warm and free from draughts. Get down on your knees and check at floor level if that is where the basket is going to be – there can be draughts around your feet that you are not aware of standing up.

Even if you intend to let your new pet roam over the whole house you should choose one room for its arrival. This should *not* be one with a door opening directly to the outside in case pussy is tempted to make a dash for 'freedom' if disturbed or panicked. It should be a room comfortable enough for you to

spend the rest of the day with the cat, but before going to bed make sure that there is nothing about which the cat could damage, or which could injure it (for during the night it may decide on a spot of exploration around the more accident-prone parts of the room, such as on table-tops and shelving). If the room has an open fireplace with a chimney you should block that up with crumpled newspaper – cats have been known to try a Father Christmas in reverse and attempt to use a chimney as an exit. A live fire should be screened behind a wire guard – and one the cat cannot get past when you have gone to bed and the fire is out, for even if it does not try to explore the chimney it may mistake the ashes for its litter and decide to use the fireplace instead of the litter tray thereafter.

The room you choose will probably not be the one in which the cat will have its litter and be fed, but for this first day bring tray and food bowls here. The kitchen, where many people decide to have them, would be far too busy for a new arrival. Once the cat has settled in you can rapidly establish the final arrangements.

Plan to bring the cat home when you have a few hours to spare in which to introduce it to its new surroundings and help it to get acclimatized. Tell friends not to visit, keep disturbance to a minimum and warn the rest of the household, especially children, that although their new friend may welcome a game it will be nervous, even perhaps a little frightened, by the upheaval and new surroundings. It will want to rest a lot and should be allowed to sleep when it decides to take a nap, though you can expect it to ask for plenty of attention first.

Other pets

If you already have other pets try to keep them out of the way for your cat's arrival. They may be delighted to have a new playmate, but at first they may also view it as an intruder to be chased off – unless the present incumbent is a hamster or guinea pig, in which case it is more likely to be shivering with fright! A new cat that at least appears to be accepted by the humans does not pose quite such a threat to an established pet – and soothe any ruffled feelings by giving the latter plenty of attention. So, keep the resident animal in another room – just at first – or get someone to take the dog out for a walk at the time you expect to arrive home.

If you are worried about another cat, as opposed to a dog, accepting the newcomer you could use the trick by which mother cats can be encouraged to accept an orphan from another litter – you make

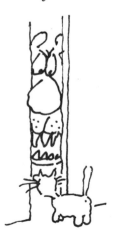

the new arrival smell like the established pet by rubbing it with a little soiled litter from the litter tray or with a blanket.

Household dangers

Having obtained the appropriate equipment and prepared your home for the cat, take a look around to see if there is anything that should *not* be there. A new cat, especially an inexperienced kitten, will want to investigate everything in its new environment. Make sure there is nothing around that could do it harm, especially if the kitten has to be left on its own from time to time. Fireplaces have already been mentioned – and you need to put gas and electric fires out of bounds as well. There should be no electricity flexes trailing about which might prove tempting playthings and could give the kitten a shock – or lead it to pull a table lamp down on its head – and in future teach it not to play with such things.

What houseplants do you have? Some very common ones are poisonous to cats: azaleas and rhododendrons, poinsettias, laurel, philodendron and dieffenbachia are all dangerous if chewed. A wide range of substances you might have in the garage, garden shed or kitchen are also poisonous, including all petroleum products, tar, paint and turpentine; many household disinfectants and bleaches; antifreeze, nicotine products and a wide range of insecticides; and, of course, all the poisons used against rats and mice. Much to the surprise of some people, who will even give one to a vase of flowers that is not in peak condition, an aspirin is very dangerous for cats – even a small amount can make them seriously ill. In fact drugs do not have the same effect on every kind of animal: morphine for example, which is used as a sedative for humans, has the opposite effect on cats and makes them very active and excited.

So, no aspirin for your cat – and no other drug without veterinary advice. Keep houseplants out of the way and perhaps offer a pot of grass instead. Cats like to eat grass from time to time and seem to know instinctively that it is good for them (see pages 47–8 for more details). The golden rule is simply to keep all poisonous substances well out of the way of an inquisitive puss – preferably in a paw-proof cabinet – and to be prepared for emergency action in the event of disaster (of which more on page 119). No one wants the old saw about curiosity killing the cat to become literally true, least of all of your pride and joy.

For the same reason, make sure that such appliances as fridges, ovens and washing machines are kept closed. It is all too easy for a nosy feline to slip inside a warm tumble dryer for a quiet snooze – until awoken at sixty revolutions per minute. Of course, you would never try to imitate the lady who took her poodle for a walk in the rain and then popped it in the microwave oven to dry (it exploded), but do get used to taking a look before you bundle in that washing and press the starter button!

Fauntleroy or Kitty?

There is one last thing to decide before you collect your cat: what are you going to call it? If it is a pedigree cat it may already have an official name, and if the name still has to be registered you may have to suggest several alternatives before you hit on one that is acceptable to the registration body and has not already been claimed – breeders often register a name (known as a 'prefix') that forms the first part of the names of all their cats. You do not *have* to call your cat by its official name, of course – Kensington Princess Aurora would be rather a mouthful anyway. You may prefer Ken, Rora or Tiddles, the name of a favourite pop star or politician, or decide that Napoleon reflects your cat's evidently bossy character. This is entirely up to you, but do choose something that is easily recognizable and simple to call.

Whatever the name you eventually select, bear in mind that one that sounds awfully clever at first could become a little embarrassing when you are calling

it loudly in the garden, or introducing the cat to visitors you are hoping to impress! You probably will, but not in the way you intend. Of course, when taking over an older cat that already knows its name, it would be much easier to stick to it than to try to teach the cat a new one.

Collection

All your preparations are complete and the big day arrives for you actually to take possession of your new cat. However tempting it may be, do not get off to a bad start by sending someone else to collect it for you. It is *you* who have to gain the cat's confidence and offer some sort of security during the traumatic experience of leaving its family and adapting to a new home. Make the journey as comfortable and as calm as possible. If it is going to be a long one, it is probably better to carry the cat in a covered basket so that it cannot peer out and so (you hope) will get bored and go to sleep. A carrier of plastic-covered wire mesh can be lined with newspaper to keep out draughts and daylight, and any basket should have several layers of newspaper in the bottom. Excitement, nerves or the sheer length of the journey would strain any cat's continence. For the same reason it is advisable not to feed the cat or give it liquids before a very long journey, nor to offer them on the way unless you are collecting from a place many hours distant. If you are, and you are travelling by car, take food, water and a litter tray with you, and keep the cat on a lead should you let it out of the basket while you stretch your legs.

Some cats enjoy travelling, watching the world through the window, but for this first trip do not take any risks. If puss complains at being shoved in a basket and then ignored, by all means respond with a little conversation – either words or cat noises, whichever comes most naturally, or least embarrassingly if travelling in public. If the basket is sufficiently open to allow through a questing paw, you might even play a game with a pencil (not a finger; those claws are sharp). Such contacts all help to build up a relationship, but at the first sign of boredom you should seize the opportunity to cover the basket and encourage the cat to sleep. Any complaining miaows from inside are best ignored.

Do not, however, even think of letting the cat roam around the car if you are driving home, especially if you wish to preserve your no-claims bonus. You cannot control the car *and* the cat at the same time. Even if you have brought someone along to look after the cat, it is tempting fate to open the basket unless the cat is already on a collar and leash and kept on very short rein. The same applies to long train journeys, as anyone who has had to catch an errant or just plain mischievous cat in a crowded compartment will testify.

The temptation to cuddle and comfort a little kitten on a journey is great, but unless you are very careful and very confident, leave it in the basket – and keep the basket shut. With an older cat this is even more important for it will be more conscious of what is happening, will have considerably more experience of getting its own way, and may fight tooth and claw not to be put back in the carrier – even if you manage to restrain it!

Arrival

When you get home, take the basket straight to the room you have selected as first base, make sure all the doors and windows are closed, and then open the basket. Let the cat venture out and explore in its own time, encouraging it to come to you. Lift it up gently and take it to the litter tray, which may be badly needed! Offer food and water, but do not worry if they are rejected for the moment – the succession of new experiences may be far too exciting to stop to think about food.

The cat will probably explore quite warily until it has assured itself there is no lurking danger, and then it may be ready for a game with a piece of string or welcome some gentle stroking. It may feel so exhausted that it just curls up for a nap, perhaps retreating back into its carrying basket, or curling up on your lap. If it settles down to a thorough wash, you can be sure it is feeling more at home.

When it falls asleep, lift it gently and put it into its own bed and let it rest, leaving food, water and litter tray all at hand.

Meeting the household

When the new arrival has settled in, the other members of the household – human and animal – can be introduced. Humans can have things explained to them and be made to wait their turn, but if you keep other cats and dogs away for long they may become jealous; they will certainly be aware that something has happened.

Do not, therefore, be tempted to let other pets in willy-nilly. Go out and make a fuss of them first, for they are

bound to be suspicious and may detect a brand-new smell on you. Let them come back into the room with you to meet the new arrival and keep your fingers crossed! If you have tried the scent-marking trick described on page 23 it may allay their worries, and they will merely be intrigued and interested by their new companion rather than sensing a threat. Even if there is a confrontation do not try to restrain them, unless the new arrival really looks in danger, for restraint only increases tension.

If an owner is very apprehensive this may be so strongly transmitted to the animals that it would be better to take the risk of leaving them alone – you can always stay within earshot should you need to intervene. Even a kitten will usually other sufficient challenge to stand its ground or, to become accepted, offer suitable submission. The established pet is often the one more frightened! Give it the most attention so that it does not feel its nose has been put out of joint. Do *not* let it see you cuddling the newcomer until they have made friends, or you may provoke a scuffle.

The rest of the human household should also give plenty of attention to any established pets and take the new arrival calmly, without fussing or pestering it. There will be plenty of time to enjoy its company later.

Settling in

Pets do not always end up the best of friends, but they usually learn to get along with one another, probably reserving some specific territory as exclusively their own – a favourite chair or sunning place, perhaps, which they expect to be vacated the moment they arrive to claim it. Sometimes an older cat, or even a dog, will be very caring and protective of a new kitten; indeed, even if they bully it at home they may defend it against outsiders. Frequently, a precocious young cat will soon start to boss an established pet about, even a hound of much larger size!

Whatever the relationship develops into, if a new kitten is allowed to snuggle up with another animal it is not likely to pine for its mother and siblings. A kitten on its own, however, will probably feel very lonely when it comes to bedtime. You could take it to bed with you – cats can make efficient warmers in cold beds on winter nights if you do not have central heating, and no one has ever heard of one getting squashed – but this could play havoc with personal relationships if you do not sleep alone. A cat rooting around deep under the bedclothes may inadvertently cause scratches in very painful places and, in any case, a cat's insistence on occupying the warmest part of the bed tends to push many partners apart.

Unless you want to establish a permanent feline bedfellow, make the kitten comfortable and then bring out the water-bottle and alarm clock. The bottle, filled with hot water, securely stoppered and wrapped in a towel or blanket so that it diffuses the heat and does not burn, provides the kitten with the warmth it used to get from its mother and brothers and sisters. Of course, a custom-made heater is even better and will give a permanently warm corner if your cat's bed is to be in a room that is otherwise unheated, but remember the warning against ordinary electric blankets. The alarm clock – the timer only wound, you do not want the bell suddenly to sound and frighten the kitten out of its fur – provides a regular and powerful thump reminiscent of the missing mother's heartbeat. Human babies respond to heartbeat rhythms too, being calmer and apparently happier, and it certainly helps to make a kitten feel secure.

Do not let the hot bottle get stone cold or it will have the reverse effect to that intended, and bury the clock beneath the bedding. Once the kitten has got used to being on its own, you can dispense with both.

Indoor exploration

When your kitten feels secure in its immediate surroundings, you can take it to explore the rest of the house. When? It may be only a matter of hours, though sometimes it can take a couple of days before an established cat and a new one are prepared to risk sharing territory. Before you let it pass through any door,

make sure all the doors and windows in the room or hall beyond are closed in case something scares the new arrival and it bolts through the nearest available opening.

Gradually introduce the kitten to the parts of the house it is to be allowed to use, but bar it firmly from any areas that are permanently out of bounds. Sooner or later it will probably find a way of sneaking into them – curiosity proving irresistible – but at least the cat will know it is not supposed to be there. Or so you hope, on the assumption that any feline trespasser will make a run for it the moment your approach is heard. And do not soften up, no matter how plaintive those miaows may sound outside the bedroom door at six o'clock in the morning. If *you* do not stick to the rules, your cat certainly won't – and you cannot begin training a kitten too soon nor postpone teaching an older cat its new household's code of conduct. But more on training soon. The new arrival's health is of greater importance.

Vet check

Top of the list of priorities, if a kitten or cat has not been immunized against feline infectious enteritis (see page 98) – and if it has you should have been given its vaccination certificate when you bought it – is a visit to the vet to have this done. At the same time the cat can have a general check-up, a sensible precaution even if it has been immunized and especially so if you have other cats at home.

Choosing a vet

How do you choose a vet? Largely by personal recommendation if you have a choice of several in your neighbourhood. Breeders may have recommendations, and you can always consult a local listings if you are really desperate or the happy-go-lucky type, but there is no substitute for word of mouth. Although a vet will do his or her best for any animal, country vets may be more expert at dealing with large farm animals than with household pets, while most city vets run small animal practices dealing mainly with cats and dogs. Among both you will find some with a particular interest in and understanding of feline medicine, and in a joint practice some partners are likely to be more felinophile than others. Do not judge a vet solely by how nice he is to you – watch how he behaves with animals.

Most cats seem to understand that a vet is really on their side, but like you they have their likes and dislikes and may trust one vet more than another – and their choice may not always be the same as yours! The appearance of the surgery, the confidence with which the vet handles your cat, and the acuteness of the questions he asks you will tell you far more about his worth than the comfort of the waiting-room or his social manner with humans.

It is often thought that vets must be on to a good thing, particularly those with fashionable practices where the fur on the owner is likely to be much more spectacular than that on the pet. Such a view may be held by the inexperienced owner presented with a sizeable bill for veterinary attention, but even a passing comparison with the much higher cost of human medicine should put things in perspective. Some vets do make a lot of money, but the work is always demanding and almost all are devoted to it. Your vet may well be annoyed if you are late for an appointment, but if necessary he would stay up all night to fight for your animal's life.

Veterinary medicine is a two-handed affair. Unless an animal is hospitalized, a vet is just as dependent on your observation and accurate reporting as on the clinical signs of the animal's present condition, so it is important that you describe symptoms as carefully as possible. It is also your responsibility to carry out the vet's instructions. If you have any doubt about the treatment you are to administer, do not hesitate to ask for explanation. A vet would much rather spend time going over points again or demonstrating things to you than to have you fail to carry them out correctly.

Veterinary bills can be high if expensive drugs and surgery are required, so you should consider taking out health insurance for your pet. Your vet will advise you on suitable schemes. For those who cannot afford to pay veterinary fees at all, animal welfare societies run free clinics in some countries, including Britain. As well as a society's own staff, other vets contribute part-time voluntary work, and you need not doubt that the societies have high medical standards. You should contribute what you can to their funds, but if you have the means to go elsewhere, do not impose on their time, which is usually in heavy demand. In any case, if you cannot afford to pay for your pet's veterinary upkeep, you should consider whether you can afford to acquire one at all.

As well as immunization against feline infectious enteritis, cats can be vaccinated against cat flu and rabies (see pages 99 and 100), although rabies vaccinations are permitted in Britain only under special circumstances.

relax after all the hard work. You cannot! The work has only just begun. It is now time to start teaching the kitten to behave in the way you want before bad habits become established that may be difficult to eradicate later.

All training depends upon understanding, encouragement and reward – not upon punishment and pain. If you make a cat afraid of you it will be unhappy and you will have no pleasure from it as a pet – quite apart from the fact that deliberate cruelty to animals is a criminal offence.

Unlike dogs, which follow the leader of their pack, a cat is unlikely to respond to simple attempts to dominate it. A cat is much more selfish and, although some of a kitten's subservience to its mother may be transferred to you as mother substitute, a cat's co-operation must be won. Associate required behaviour with food, physical pleasures such as stroking, and with appreciative and friendly sounds.

Training techniques

Your kitten looks happy and healthy and appears to have settled into its new home. You now eye that comfy chair and think that perhaps you can afford to

Whenever possible, discouragement should be dissociated from the owner. A squirt from a water-pistol (or a plastic bottle with a nozzle of the kind that holds washing-up liquid), a shot from a pea-shooter, or a dried pea flicked by finger and thumb can be dissuasive and not immediately linked with teacher. In that way the lesson learned is general and good behaviour will not depend on your always being there to ensure it.

If a direct reproof is necessary, a gentle tap on the nose or a blow near by (missing the cat) with a roll of newspaper should be enough to stop a cat from pestering for food at the table or jumping up on to it. But take warning: some cats will happily put up with such small-scale discomfort and turn the whole thing into a game – *their* action triggering *your* response. If this happens, and unless you actually want the cat to start bossing you about, change tactics by, for example, shutting it out of the room at mealtimes.

It is essential that you (and the rest of the household) stick to your rules, otherwise you will either confuse the cat or encourage it to believe it can get away with murder. A cat's resource and cunning are part of its attraction, and many owners are tremendously impressed at the skill with which their cat regularly outwits them – but you are in for a hard time if your cat decides you actually admire its misdemeanours. In fact, you are in for anarchy. Cats are very responsive to tone of voice and easily recognize displeasure, but if you try to sound annoyed while actually laughing at their effrontery you cannot expect them to take you seriously.

Teaching a name

You will want your cat to come when called and to know when it is being spoken to. It does not usually take long for kittens to learn to respond to their names, but for an older cat, no doubt set in its ways, learning a new name may be more difficult. Use a cat's name when you are putting food down and when it comes to eat, and when you are stroking it and playing with it. You thereby hope that the cat will associate its name with pleasant things. For this reason, some people advise against ever using a cat's name when correcting it – just say 'bad cat' or something similar (depending, of course, on whether you are in front of the children and how annoyed you happen to be).

When a cat comes to you, always offer a titbit or some special petting in the earlier training period, so rewarding its response. By the time it is trained, you will probably find you are greeting it as you would any friend, although do not make the mistake of thinking it will agree with absolutely everything you say!

Do not, on the other hand, try to train a cat to come to you just after it has had a meal or when it is about to curl up for a nap. You will almost certainly fail, because the cat will inevitably conclude, especially with a full stomach, that there is no need to pay you the least attention. To begin with, call a cat only when it is going to *want* to come to you. Such a tactic may be taking the line of least resistance, but it is the way to build up the right response.

Toilet-training

Most kittens are toilet-trained by their mothers, and you need do no more than show them the litter tray, place them on it and perhaps move their paws in a digging action. It is usually easy to tell when a kitten is about to defecate or urinate: it will adopt a pose with its rear held off the ground. If it is in the wrong place, pick it up gently and place it in the right one. Do not act too suddenly or the kitten may pee from fright.

If a cat soils outside its litter tray it will seldom do so deliberately, although cats have been known to do this in order to attract attention to something else. The usual cause is that the litter needs changing and has become unacceptable, or has been placed somewhere awkward or uncomfortable.

Clean a soiled place thoroughly or the scent left behind will encourage the cat to use it again. Swabbing with vinegar will help to disguise any remaining smell and also seems to put cats off. If the cat persists in going to a particular spot, try placing the litter tray there for a day or so. Then, having made sure that the cat uses the tray, move it a short distance towards its correct location after every visit. Your guests may find the household rather odd, but that is better than driving them all away because the house reeks of urine!

There is no point in rubbing a cat's nose in a soiled area or in chastising a cat after the event. That would risk associating your displeasure with what the cat is doing at the time. It is clear, however, that many cats are aware of their 'mis-demeanour', especially if their attention is drawn to it, and that it causes them distress. Untypical failure to use the litter tray may be an indication of a urinary disorder or other illness (see page 91) and warrants consultation with a vet.

All cats should be litter-trained, for even if they are to be allowed outdoors there may be times when they have to be restricted to the house because of sickness or because they are on heat, or they may simply not want to go out in bad weather. However, if you can encourage a cat to perform its natural functions outside (providing this is safe, of course) you will save yourself the chore of changing litter. This may make *you* happy, but possibly not your neighbours should puss decide to dig a spacious latrine in their herbaceous border.

Initially, a litter-trained cat will still come back to the tray even when allowed outdoors. The easiest way of encouraging a cat to transfer from the litter tray to the garden entirely is to take the tray outside. At first change the litter as usual, then, when the cat is used to the new location, remove the tray and simply leave a small pile of litter, which can be reduced gradually as the outdoor location becomes established.

Spraying

Spraying a place with urine is part of feline territorial marking (see page 60) and is quite distinct from bad toilet-training. It does not occur in kittens or females, and rarely with males neutered before sexual maturity. However, even neutered males may sometimes spray when under stress or when, for example, overcrowding makes it difficult for them to establish individual territories. A water-pistol or similar 'dissociated punishment' (see page 30) may be effective if used when a cat is actually spraying, but it is extremely difficult to stop such instinctive behaviour – one very good reason for neutering toms not required for breeding.

Scratching

Damage to furniture, carpets and curtains can be a frequent problem with an untrained cat. Like spraying, it is a means of claiming territory: particular sites are repeatedly scratched and scent marks from the paws deposited at the same time. Outdoors this may occur on trees and posts, indoors on your furniture or perhaps a doorway. Once a particular place has become established as a marking site, it can be extremely

difficult to transfer the attention elsewhere. For a cat, scent-marking is like running up a flag to declare one's territorial rights; and the markings must be continually refreshed.

If a scratching habit develops indoors it should rapidly be redirected to a piece of furniture you are prepared to sacrifice (and to keep around in a mutilated state) or, preferably, to a special scratching-post or panel. For cats kept indoors, one or the other will be essential: in addition to the marking procedure, all cats need to stretch their claws, and the indoor cat must have somewhere to do so. This exercise also removes the old, outer covering of the front claws when it gets worn to reveal the sharp new points beneath.

A scratching-post or panel (see page

21) can be bought ready-made, or made yourself. It should be heavy enough so that the cat cannot pull it over, or fixed to a base on which the cat can stand when stretching. Alternatively, it can be fitted firmly beneath a horizontal surface, such as a work-top or the treads of an open stair. If you make your own, cover it in a coarse material not found elsewhere in the house so that your curtains or fabric-textured walls cannot be confused with it. Introduce a new kitten or cat to the site by holding its front paws against the post or panel and moving them through the scratching motion. The lesson will probably not need to be repeated – just keep an eye open to prevent scratching anywhere else.

It may be that your cat has already chosen a place to scratch – and not one you approve. You will stand a better chance of persuading it to scratch where *you* want if you cover the post or panel with material of the same texture. If your cat wrecks the carpet rather than an upright surface, you should mount your scratching-panel horizontally on the floor in a fairly damage-resistant part of the house. Do not mount the panel actually on the carpet itself, or the surrounding area will just get scratched to pieces as well.

Some owners finally lose patience with their cat's scratching activities and ask the vet to de-claw it. This involves removing the claws and the ends of the bones from which they grow, so taking away the cat's ability to grip surfaces and the weapons it needs for self-defence. No one who even thinks of having such a barbaric operation carried out should keep a cat: it is cruel and unnecessary, and scratching is anyway quite instinctive.

Reforming a gourmet

Changing a kitten's diet to that of an adult cat, or changing an adult's from what it has had before to something more convenient – introducing canned or other proprietary foods, for example – is not 'training' as such, but still requires a disciplined approach on your part. Provided you are sure you are offering suitable food, and there are no digestive problems that may make a cat refuse it, change will be largely a matter of persistence on your part. Except with very young kittens, it will not hurt a cat occasionally to go without a meal, so if perfectly good food is refused do not offer an alternative. Puss may prefer smoked salmon, but has to learn that it is no longer on the menu. Remove the food if it begins to get dirty or dried out, but offer more of the same at the next mealtime. The cat may still turn up its nose – probably by scratching around as though the food were in the litter tray, a very clear sign of what it thinks – but it is quite likely to creep back for a snack when you are not looking.

Even the most pampered cat can be taught to eat what is offered if you are sufficiently firm. This will make life easier for you and especially so for your bank manager. The difficulty comes with an older cat that has been fed a very particular diet and looks with horror at your

cat, which does not want a rumbling stomach any more than you do.

Cat-flaps

Some cats have to go out from time to time, and most others would certainly like to. In the absence of a butler, there are two ways to deal with this. The first is to train the cat to come and go at regular times and then open the door whenever it calls (naturally, you hope these times will be of your own choosing. Some hope!). The second is to install the cat's own door, small enough to let it through but not a burglar – and much safer than leaving a window open.

Cat doors usually have a swinging panel to seal the opening and hence are known as 'cat-flaps'. Free-swinging ones tend to let in draughts and so are made with one flap inside another; one swings outwards and one inwards. They are usually fitted with some sort of catch or bolt so they can be locked closed if a female is in season or if for some other reason you want to restrict the cat's movements. A cat-flap can be set into a hole in the wall, in a door panel or even into a pane of glass in the window – but always be sure that it is far enough away from locks and catches to discourage a long-armed burglar from reaching through.

To train a cat to use a flap, wedge it open (the flap, not the cat) for a period and show the cat the opening. To get the cat used to the arrangement, put it outside and then call it back indoors for

bowl of proprietary titbits. The best way of breaking this impasse is to introduce new foodstuffs gradually by mixing them a little at a time with the established diet, in the hope that kitty will not catch on and eventually may even come to like your new provisions. This rather underhand tactic usually works but be prepared for the occasional set-back: even humans can spot frozen cod masquerading as a fresh trout.

Changes from fresh foods to canned, or from canned to dry or semi-moist preparations, should always be made gradually so the cat's digestion can adapt to the new diet. Do not withhold alternatives in these cases: it is not fair on the meals so that it has to jump through the opening to get at its food. Next, try doing this with the flap down, and if the cat does not immediately try to push it open, show it how easy this is to do. Most cats will learn quite rapidly – and by now they will probably be hungry, too.

Many cat-flaps, however, suffer from an irritating drawback: other cats may learn to use them as well, whether your cat's guests or intruders. An 'entire' (unneutered) tom, for example, is likely to leave a visiting card, more probably a series of them, to remind you of its call for many days afterwards. The answer is to give your cat its own key. One type of cat-flap uses a battery-operated electromagnet, activated by a small magnet on the cat's collar, to open or lock the flap. Provided every cat in the neighbourhood does not have this luxury the device works well, and if you have several cats in the household then all can have their personal magnet. Unfortunately, since magnets have only two poles, only two types of key are possible – and a neighbouring cat with a magnet of the same polarity as yours will find that its key fits your lock; just hope this is not a smelly and delinquent tom.

Lead-training

Sometimes, especially in a city, it is not safe to let a cat go out on its own. If this applies to you, then consider teaching your cat to walk on a lead – a discipline that is not very common among cats, but which can be extremely useful. A cat

may choose to follow its owner and some will trail along behind any friendly human, but cats are not naturally led, as dogs are, so teaching them to walk on a lead is much more difficult. The best chance of success lies in starting very young and capitalizing on the way kittens follow their mother.

Once used to its collar, the kitten can be introduced to the lead, which should not be presented as another string-like plaything to be pounced upon. You can try distracting the kitten's attention from it by playing with a piece of string at the same time, but you must give the kitten the opportunity to establish that the lead is something safe.

After attaching the lead, do not let the kitten drag it around – always take the weight at the other end. Call the kitten to you, drawing on the lead to prevent it going slack as the kitten gets closer. Then follow the kitten's movements, at first still facing it to give encouragement if that is necessary, but after a while with your back to it. Always praise the cat when it does what you want, but do not risk reproving it lest this be misunderstood and connected with the very action you are trying to develop.

Few cats are successfully lead-trained, perhaps because their owner starts too late or does not persist for long enough. Even some professional trainers have had little luck. As with all training, frequent short sessions are much more effective than protracted ones that can become boring for both parties: a few minutes *every* day is better than an hour on Saturdays.

Do not be dismayed if you fail in your attempt to teach the cat to come for a walk with you. You may console yourself with the thought that such independence is preferable to the over-excited canine behaviour that occurs every time 'walkies' is mentioned. And even partial familiarity with a lead may prove useful on those occasions when you do not want to confine your cat in a basket but nevertheless need to restrain it from rushing off in fright or pursuing its own investigations.

If you are one of the lucky successful trainers, consider changing the collar for a harness, which avoids putting undue strain upon the neck. A very small kitten-size harness may be difficult to obtain, although some very small dog harnesses are made, but you should have little trouble in acquiring one for a fully grown cat.

Clever kitty

If you can train your cat to use a lead, you can probably teach it anything from fetching your paper to lighting your cigarette, though doing the washing-up may be rejected as too demeaning.

The key to teaching a cat to do anything is to exploit its natural feline actions and build upon things you have seen it do already. For example, if you want your cat to jump through a hoop, you should first get it used to walking through the hoop on the floor and then gradually raise the hoop from the ground, perhaps by placing it on the edge

of a familiar chair. Such a circus act, however, might be thought rather eccentric by most cat owners, and probably by most cats, too. On the other hand, some cats will fail to comprehend even a simple action if you try to teach it to them, but will have no difficulty learning much more complex ones for themselves by watching you. Many is the owner who has tried in vain to teach kitty how to hook a paw round the edge of a door, only to see it leap up and try to turn the knob.

Playtime

Cats will often invent games for you to play with them. Anything that moves or hides – you, your finger, a piece of string, a pencil – can become a plaything. But you should remember that a cat's claws and teeth can be very sharp indeed, and although most cats are extremely gentle with those they like, and would not deliberately injure them, the excitement of the game may overcome their usual restraint and lead to painful scratches – for which you can hardly blame the cat.

Cats especially like anything they can chase, or that rustles or makes an interesting but not loud noise. Crumpled paper, small plastic balls (those with a sort of trellis-work shell can be more easily tossed than table-tennis balls, and still ricochet off a wall) or anything with a human at the other end will give pleasure. Some cats will retrieve: carrying things in their mouth is a natural action, and if they realize that by bringing something back to you it will be thrown again so they can chase after it, they will probably teach *you* to play. No doubt they conclude that you are bored and in need of diversion, and bring you a ball so that you can amuse yourself by throwing it. Some cats have developed this into a fine art, sitting quite still in the middle of the room while the hapless owner scurries around after the ball. No wonder some of them seem to think that their owners are eccentric!

3. Keeping your cat contented

A domestic cat would find it very difficult to fend for itself. Feral cats, especially in cities, rely heavily on scavenging and supplementary human feeding, but their needs still reflect those of the wild cat. Now that you have taken on the responsibility of meeting them, you need to understand them properly.

Filling the family tiger's tank

The cat is a meat-eater and its digestive system is not designed to handle a lot of vegetable matter; meat or fish form its principal diet. A cat's body simply cannot extract the right nutrients from vegetable foods, and whereas we – and our dogs – get most of our energy needs from carbohydrates, a cat cannot so easily digest them. Cats need protein to fuel their energy reserves; and protein means meat.

This does not necessarily mean the best fillet steak, however. In the wild, a cat would eat the whole of a carcass – guts and all – and so obtain essential vitamins and minerals. If you pamper your pet with prime steak, these will be missing, and must be provided with supplements. Fortunately, most pet food manufacturers have researched the cat's needs and produce carefully balanced foods that have all the right constituents.

However, even though your cat may, like those in the advertisements, decide that a particular brand is its favourite

food, you should not give the same product all the time. Cats can become very fussy eaters and, when over-indulged in a particular taste, may refuse to try something unfamiliar later, so offer a range of foods. Otherwise, if a commercial brand goes off the market or changes its recipe, or if a source of fresh food becomes unavailable, you could be in for a frustrating time.

If you are feeding a large number of cats, fresh foods prepared in bulk may prove more economical, but the convenience and reliability of proprietary foods makes them the obvious choice for many people – but you should feed fresh food too, perhaps one day each week. Encourage cats to take semi-moist and dry foods as well.

Most cats seem to be convinced that 'the other bowl is always tastier' and that stolen food is tastiest of all. The skill with which some cats will snatch a steak from right under your nose may gain your admiration, but if food is given from table or thieving encouraged you will not only find such behaviour difficult to stop but may find it much more difficult to get a cat to take interest in the food you officially provide.

Feeding patterns

Always offer food at regular times and in the same place. Do not serve it outdoors, where it is likely to be exposed to flies and go off more rapidly. The adult cat may be satisfied with only one meal each day, but most owners prefer to feed in the morning and evening. Pregnant and nursing females and young cats need to be fed more often (see pages 82 and 88).

Kittens should be given their food in four or five meals daily, reducing to three by the time they are about nine months old. For their size, kittens need much more food than adult cats, for it must provide for growth as well as maintaining their physique and supplying energy. Recently weaned kittens need about 20 per cent of their own body weight in fresh or canned food each day, dropping to about 9 per cent when they are about six months old, and to as little as 6 per cent for an active adult cat.

Canned and fresh food contains a great deal of moisture, so quantities will be accordingly less for semi-moist and dry foods. Even with the most moist of food always have a bowl of fresh water available – and if you feed dry foods, check that the water is actually drunk, for it is absolutely essential for the cat's health. The quantities recommended by pet food manufacturers give you a reasonable guide. For some cats they may err on the generous side and, if your cat fails to eat all that is given, it may be more than it needs. The best guide to correct food intake is when a cat not only seems healthy, but maintains a consistent weight. The table on page 45 gives an approximate guide for a variety of foods.

Opposite: *The Seal Point Siamese is elegant, talkative and makes an excellent companion.*

Opposite, above left: *The Chinchilla, one of the most beautiful of Longhairs.*

Opposite, above right: *A thickset tabby? Actually the European wild cat, probably an ancestor of the domestic cat.*

Opposite below: *Seal Point Birmans, long-haired cats that have Siamese-like points but white paws.*

Above: *Abyssinian cats, with their ticked fur, are intelligent and notably inquisitive.*

Average daily food requirements for your cat

Type of cat	Cat's weight	Canned food	Semi-moist food	Dry food
Kitten				
3 months	14½ oz - 2 lb 6 oz (0.5 - 1.1 kg)	2¾ - 7 oz (77 - 196 g)	1 - 2¾ oz (28 - 77 g)	1 - 2½ oz (28 - 70 g)
6 months	3 lb 2 oz - 5 lb 8 oz (1.4 - 2.5 kg)	4½ - 7¾ oz (125 - 216 g)	1¾ - 3 oz (49 - 84 g)	1½ - 2½ oz (42 - 70 g)
Lazy cat	4 lb 13 oz - 9 lb 15 oz (2.2 - 4.5 kg)	4½ - 9 oz (126 - 252 g)	1¾ - 3½ oz (49 - 98 g)	1½ - 3¼ oz (42 - 90 g)
Active cat	4 lb 13 oz - 9 lb 15 oz (2.2 - 4.5 kg)	5¼ - 11 oz (148 - 305 g)	2 - 4¼ oz (56 - 120 g)	2 - 3¾ oz (56 - 105 g)
Pregnant cat	5 lb 8 oz - 8 lb 13 oz (2.5 - 4 kg)	7 - 11½ oz (200 - 322 g)	2¾ - 4½ oz (77 - 126 g)	2½ - 4 oz (70 - 112 g)
Nursing cat	4 lb 13 oz - 8 lb 13 oz (2.2 - 4 kg)	15¾ - 28½ oz (442 - 800 g)	6¼ - 11½ oz (175 - 322 g)	5½ - 10 oz (155 - 280 g)

A cat that spends a lot of time asleep may still have a high metabolic rate and thus need more food than is suggested here for an inactive animal. A nursing mother may eat as much as two large tins of cat food a day. For an active cat of average weight, between half and three-quarters of a large tin will be plenty — so do not worry if your cat eats somewhat less than the label on the can suggests.

But how are you going to weigh your cat? Do not try to suspend it by its collar from a spring balance, nor expect it to sit quietly in a pan while you pile up the necessary weights. With a small and fairly co-operative cat, put it in a cardboard box and place it on the kitchen scales. Then weigh the box empty. The difference between the two will be the weight of the cat. Alternatively, you may find it more convenient (and easier for handling a less co-operative cat) to hold the cat while you stand on your bathroom scales, then let the cat jump down, check your own weight – and work out the difference. The kitchen scales will probably have more accurate calibration, but the bathroom technique still gives a reasonable guide – even if it is a nagging reminder to watch your own weight!

Opposite: Lack of a pedigree won't stop this kitten from growing up to be a delightful pet.

Fresh foods

The first rule is variety. Muscle meat or boned fish lack calcium and vitamin A. An excess of oily fish leads to loss of vitamin E, and a great deal of horsemeat will have the same effect. Too much liver produces an excess of vitamin A, which builds up until it poisons the system.

Milk will supply calcium (about a teacupful each day contains sufficient) and is a natural food for all young mammals. However, many adult cats cannot digest it and it produces diarrhoea and flatulence. They can be given a calcium supplement instead. Yeast tablets, which all cats will benefit from, provide vitamin B, and multi-vitamin and mineral supplements are also available.

Raw meat can occasionally be given if absolutely fresh – except for pork, which should be well-cooked since it is more likely to carry tapeworm – but remember that that tasty looking slice of steak may have been in the butcher's for several days. In general it is better to serve meat lightly cooked in order to kill any germs, but not too cooked – overcooking destroys vitamin B1. On the other hand, an enzyme in raw fish also destroys this vitamin, so always serve fish lightly cooked, too.

Some cats enjoy gnawing on a bone or will even crunch up small bones if given the chance (they seem instinctively aware of their need for calcium), but generally speaking all meat and fish should be served with the bones removed. Take care that no sharp splinters of bone or pieces softened by cooking (as in a stew) remain, for they can easily become skewered on the teeth, causing considerable consternation on the part of the cat and possible injury if you inexpertly try to remove them. Other small bones can become wedged in the mouth or throat.

Vegetables and cereals must be cooked if a cat is to digest them, and should not form more than about one-fifth of the total volume of food. They will provide bulk but, although some cats show a liking for particular delicacies – like one Siamese that relished mushrooms and asparagus tips – others refuse vegetable and cereals altogether, even when cunningly disguised with meat and gravy.

Most cats occasionally eat grass, and some show a passion for it. It probably provides roughage in the diet, and also appears to act as an emetic to help the regurgitation of fur-balls produced from fur swallowed when licking the coat. A cat without access to grass will often eat similar-looking plants, such as the leaves of crocus or spider plants, which will simply make it sick – and some are poisonous too (see page 23). If you do not have a lawn, at least make sure that some grass is growing somewhere in the garden. For indoor cats, grow a pot of grass specially for them. However, to avoid any misunderstanding with the Drug Squad, remember that cocksfoot (*Dactylis glomerata*) is one type that cats seem to like.

Eggs are rich in protein, fat, and vitamins, and are a useful occasional addition to any diet. Serve them lightly cooked (raw egg white destroys biotin, one of the B group of vitamins). Chopped boiled egg or scrambled egg is probably easiest for a cat to enjoy.

Some cats like the occasional piece of cheese, and very often the smellier the better. In this respect they can beat off competition from any would-be gourmandizer.

Warning: If you feed your cat table scraps, beware of any prepared meats that contain preservative. Check the label to see what kind, if any, is used and if the chemical is not specified you should keep an eye on the cat's reaction to the snack – and never feed it again if puss seems uneasy. One commonly used preservative is benzoic acid, which produces aggressive behaviour in cats and sometimes causes hyperactivity.

Commercial cat foods

Some pet foods are composed entirely of meat or fish. Frequently they are presented as 'gourmet' food for cats, with a price to match. Like fresh meat on its own, however, they will not provide a balanced diet, although they will make an occasional treat. The manufacturers have put years of dietary research into their cat food recipes. The label should give some guide to their content, and will probably state that they provide all that a cat requires. But do watch out for optimistic-sounding claims. If a brand presents itself as having 'pure beef added', what else is lurking inside? Bulk for bulk, canned cat foods are more expensive than dog foods. That is because dog foods contain cheaper vegetable protein. Do not try to economize by feeding your cat dog food – it will not give the right balance, even if puss steals it from Rover's bowl.

Semi-moist foods, sold in foil bags, and dried foods are not as readily taken by all cats, and you may have great difficulty getting an older cat to accept them at all if they have not been a regular part of its diet. On the other hand, some cats clearly prefer them.

The dried foods have the advantage that they can be left down all day without going off, especially if in a covered feeder. When they were first introduced, their mineral balance, together with a lack of moisture content, led to urinary blockages in some cats. Manufacturers of reputable makes adjusted their recipes and also added extra salt to encourage the cat to drink more. They are now considered quite safe provided the cat takes plenty of water, so check that the water bowl is always full. For young cats being fed semi-moist foods, milk should also be offered.

Both semi-moist and dry foods have a shelf life of about six months. Dry foods will keep after opening if served daily and not allowed to become damp. They will keep dry if transferred to a tin with a tight lid.

The best plan is to offer a diet to match your pocket, formed from all kinds of proprietary products and fresh food, which can be butcher's offal, fish heads, and so on, so that the cat does not become conditioned to a particular type.

Treats

While you should not let your cat get faddy over food, an occasional treat will do no harm. Despite its carnivorous nature, a cat's favourite food will not necessarily be meat. A predilection for grass has already been mentioned, and specific types of grass may particularly please certain cats, but their variety in taste is boundless. One cat loving a flavour that another dislikes can be a boon in a household where a particular cat tries to get the lion's share of everything on offer.

Here are just a few things that one family's cats have fancied: asparagus tips, processed cheese, sausage (but not salami), smoked salmon (preferably Scotch), food flakes and pellets for goldfish, lightly fried mushrooms, liver pâté, marshmallows, Marmite, cornflakes with milk, prawns (or preferably lobster, if available), French beans (cooked), spaghetti (uncooked), dry champagne, and, in the case of a Siamese that did *not* drink milk, cream – not lapped but licked from a paw that had been dipped into the jug. Yet not one of these cats liked any of the proprietary sweets that are sold as 'kitten treats'!

The serving of champagne, incidentally, or any other alcoholic drink, is frankly to be discouraged. Alcohol has a drastic enough effect on most humans, and your cat will not appreciate a hangover.

Fragrant felines

Grooming

All cats wash themselves – well, almost all; there are one or two that seem to prefer to rely on their fellows to do it for them – but this does not relieve you of the task of grooming to keep their coats in good condition. It will not only help to keep the cat clean and healthy, but will keep hairs off your furnishings as well. Do not think the occasional visit to an expensive pussy parlour will let you off the chore (if you have such establishments in your part of town). Unless the chauffeur takes the cat round every day, someone will still be lumbered with the job – or have you got staff to spare? You certainly need a healthy private income to keep on paying for a de luxe wash and set.

Grooming should start in early kittenhood. It gets the kitten used to being handled and encourages the fur to grow in the way it should. An older cat, not used to a proper grooming, may be uncooperative and even scratch or bite at first, but most cats enjoy the attention, just as we might enjoy a scalp massage or having someone brush our hair.

A difficult cat requires the indirect approach. Sidle up when it is sitting quietly, perhaps snoozing, and groom it a little – stopping the moment it shows any annoyance. You should gradually be able to gain its confidence and co-operation. Many cats object to having their stomach brushed or even tickled though others love it. For the latter it is a reminder of licking by their mother, one of their earliest sensations. If grooming carries on directly from the mother's care or, better, overlaps it, the kitten will grow up considering it a pleasurable and reassuring practice, which is why an early start to the routine is important. If you let a cat or kitten lie on your lap and stroke it under the chin, then right down its belly, it may soon get used to being handled in this way.

Equipment
This consists of a brush and either a comb with both wide and very close-set teeth, or two combs. The brush should have natural bristles rather than wire or plastic, which may tug fur out at the roots, or nylon, which will produce static electricity. Rex cats need a very soft brush because they lack guard hairs, and a rubber brush (really a pad with rubber knobs) is good for many Shorthairs. The

wide comb is for normal combing, the other for removing dirt and possible fleas or ticks. A piece of silk, velvet or chamois leather is also useful, and some people use talcum powder, fuller's earth or similar proprietary powders to give a dry shampoo and absorb grease – especially if preparing a cat for a show. Cologne is another possible grease remover. It rather depends on how pampered you want your cat to be.

Cotton buds will be useful, and for an indoor cat get a pair of nail-clippers for cutting the claws (see page 52). Never try to cut a cat's claws with scissors, though they will be useful if you need to cut out fur snags or hair that has picked up paint or similar substances.

Long-haired cats
These should be groomed daily – frequent grooming keeps the coat in an easily manageable state and will take up less time than trying to cope with tangles and snags that develop if you neglect your duty.

Ideally, spread a sheet of paper on a table and groom the cat on this. Newspaper is not ideal because the object is to be able to identify the dirt and any parasites that fall out, and for this you need clean white paper. Even if your cat prefers to be groomed on your lap, try to do it on a table fairly frequently for this reason.

Start with a general inspection to check there are no wounds and that the mouth looks healthy: no broken teeth, build-up of tartar or bad breath. Clean the eyes with a piece of cotton wool (absorbent cotton) dampened in warm water. Wipe down and towards the nose and then gently outwards. To clean the ears use cotton buds on sticks (never use them for the eyes – it is too easy to poke the eye) moistened with baby oil or rubbing alcohol (surgical spirit), checking them for infection. There should be a little golden wax in the ear canal, but if it is a dirty brown or produces an unpleasant odour it is almost certainly a sign of ear mites (see page 108).

Now, begin to comb the cat, looking out for parasites as you do so and checking the skin condition. The fine-toothed comb will trap fleas that have not fled before it and will remove the tell-tale black specks of their droppings. If in doubt you can distinguish flea droppings from dirt by pressing them with a damp cloth – flea droppings will leave a blood-coloured smudge. First comb the legs, then the belly flanks and back. Work vertically upwards and from front to back. The open-toothed comb will deal with loose tangles, or they can be teased out with the fingers: a knitting needle or thin skewer can sometimes help. Really obstinate tangles and snags will have to be cut out with scissors. Avoid tugging at the fur – think how painful it is if someone pulls *your* hair!

If secretions from the sebaceous glands around the base of the tail have stained a light-coloured coat, a powdering with talc may help to absorb the grease. When this becomes a serious problem, as it sometimes does in males, it is usually known as 'stud tail' and will require veterinary attention.

General dry shampoos can be given with talc or other powders, are dusted into the coat right down to the roots and rubbed into the fur with the tips of the fingers, before being thoroughly brushed and combed out. Since it is not easy to remove every particle of powder or talc, pale materials should not be used on black or very dark cats lest everyone thinks your pride and joy is rife with dandruff. For dark-coated cats, bran warmed in the oven is often used for a dry shampoo and is available from many pet stores. If the cat is placed in a box with the bran in the bottom it makes application easier.

Normal-size brushes are not suitable for brushing facial hair, so use a soft toothbrush. Brush the ruff and face hair so that they stand out from the head.

Short-haired cats

The short-haired breeds do not need so much time spent on grooming. The method is the same as for Longhairs, except that combing and brushing should be from front to back in a horizontal direction – though some cats, especially Siamese, seem to enjoy having their fur brushed in all directions and a vigorous scalp massage with the fingertips from someone who has gained their confidence.

Simple hand-grooming (heavy stroking) will remove quite a lot of loose hairs, particularly after a massage against the lie of the fur. After brushing, a rub in the same direction with a pad of velvet or chamois leather will add an extra polish to short fur, and a clean piece of old nylon stocking pulled over the brush so that the bristles poke through adds an extra gloss to long fur on

its final brushing. Always comb the hair off brushes after use, and keep both brushes and combs well washed.

Shampooing

Wet shampoos may sometimes be necessary. Start when the kitten is young so it gets used to the idea. If you know your cat hates being washed and it is necessary to bathe it, do not let it see you making the preparations! You do not want it fighting even before the battle begins.

Do not use human adult shampoos on cats – special cat shampoo formulas or very mild baby shampoos are as strong as cats can tolerate. You will find it easier to use the kitchen sink or a washbasin than the bathtub: they are at a much more convenient height for you to control the cat.

Do not expect a cat to like being submerged in water, or to tolerate having water poured over it without reaction. Have a bowl ready-filled to a depth of about 4 in (10 cm) at a temperature comfortable to your elbow, as for a baby's bath. Wear gloves, especially if your cat is not used to bathing (not to keep your hands dry, but to protect them from the cat). An extra pair of hands to help will also speed up the job, making it much easier to accomplish.

1. Holding the cat firmly, put it in the bowl. Wet its head first and then the rest of it.

2. Work up a lather with the shampoo, taking care to keep the soap well away from the cat's eyes.

3. Pull the plug and rinse the cat with a

hand-held shower spray or, if that is not possible, have a second bowl of lukewarm water standing ready for the rinse. If a medicated shampoo is given a rinse may be inappropriate; follow the directions of your vet or of the shampoo manufacturer.

4. Dry the cat briskly by wrapping it in a rough towel. If the cat will tolerate a hair-dryer, finish off the drying with that, set only to warm (not hot) and not held very close. Groom as you dry. Whether after a shampoo or recovering from an accidental soaking, brushing will help speed drying. Keep the cat well out of draughts until the fur is absolutely dry.

If a cat gets a little paint, tar or similar substance on its coat or paws you may be able to loosen it by liberally swabbing it with cooking or olive oil (if you can, actually dip the affected area in the oil). If less firmly attached, washing rapidly with washing-up liquid may do the trick. Always rinse well afterwards.

Claw-trimming

Cats, especially those kept indoors, that do not get much exercise on hard and rough surfaces often grow their claws more quickly than they wear them down. When claws become too long they begin to curve backwards and must be trimmed. With a trusting cat and a pair of clippers (the kind for human nails that look rather like a pair of wire-cutters are best – do not try using scissors) this is not difficult. Begin trimming when the cat is still a kitten to get it used to the idea. Dealing with an older cat for the first few times or with any cat that does not like being handled may require help from someone else to hold the animal. Only cut the claws in good light so you can easily see the pink quick, the still-live part where there are blood vessels, for you must *not* cut near this area.

Hold a paw in one hand and squeeze it gently so the claws are extended. Align the clipper blades to the sides of the claw, and squeeze the clippers firmly. Stop if the cat shows any sign of pain, which means you are not doing it correctly. If you have any doubts about trimming

claws, ask your vet to do it for you, or to show you how it should be done.

Only cut a cat's claws if they grow too long. Claw-trimming will not stop a cat from scratching, and it may even increase the activity to sharpen the trimmed ends.

Travelling with your cat

Travelling baskets, leads and the need to have complete control over your cat when travelling have already been discussed in Chapter 2. It is wise to avoid feeding for about six hours before a long journey. To reduce the stress upon the cat, and especially if for some reason you are forced to send a cat without anyone to look after it, your vet may recommend some type of sedative for the journey.

Cats do not normally suffer from travel sickness (though there are exceptions); they seem to have a more developed sense of balance than dogs and humans, which can be car-, sea- and air-sick, due to a different structure in the inner ear.

Railways, bus companies, ships, and airlines – all have their own regulations for the transportation of pets. Most stipulate that a cat should be in an enclosed container. Taxis may also refuse to carry animals, although they are unlikely to refuse a cat if it is in a carrying basket. Airlines often do not allow animals to travel with the passengers.

A well-behaved pet that trusts you is an easier proposition. On a long car journey, for example, there is unlikely to be much risk in letting it out of its carrier and asking a back-seat passenger to look after it. It will be able to share the journey, watch the world through the window and curl up on a friendly lap. Keep it on a short leash, however, do not let it climb up behind the driver (a playful paw across the face could mean trouble at a busy intersection) and never let it travel in the front of a car where it can interfere with the controls. This is especially important in the racier model of automobile with touch-sensitive instrumentation.

Cats may enjoy the attention they get from other passengers on public transport, but it is still advisable to keep them in their carrier. If you let your cat out, even if you keep it on a lead, you may have difficulty in preventing it from crawling under bus seats or attempting to explore a railway carriage. Great care is required in such circumstances and it is better not to take the risk. And this applies only to cautious and normally well-behaved cats; those of independent temperament are virtually bound to cause trouble if given the opportunity to do so.

In any case, for the sake of your cat's health you should try to avoid contact with other people or animals on public transport. Either may be carriers of infection and a cat which is usually kept indoors may not have developed resistance even to quite minor diseases. On most public transport systems you will not be allowed to take the cat out of its carrier, anyway.

An unaccompanied animal must be supplied with good ventilation, a tray of litter (or a thick layer of newspaper for a short journey), a piece of blanket to make a bed and, for a long journey, a supply of water. Arrangements should be made for the railway guard, or bus or ship's crew, to check the cat at intervals. Over very long journeys of more than twenty-four hours they would have to be responsible for food, water, and litter as well, which means that advance preparation on your part is essential. Containers should be clearly labelled with the name, address and telephone number of both sender and recipient.

A home away from home

If you take your cat away for weekends or for holidays, do not risk losing it. There are famous and well-documented cases of cats finding their way home, or tracing their owners over considerable distances (see page 66), but do not bank on yours being one of these super-cats. Some cats learn quickly that they have a second, weekend territory, and, because they have a good sense of time, learn not to wander far at the hour you normally leave for home – but do not put off calling them until you are ready to depart. If a cat is busy on a hunting expedition, it may be extremely reluctant to nip back home, especially with a tiresome journey in prospect.

A different environment may produce some surprising changes in a cat. A lethargic, apartment-bound animal may reveal itself as an accomplished hunter when let loose in the countryside, returning home with a rabbit as large as itself in its jaws and displaying an independence and self-sufficiency that is quite unlike its city behaviour. However, be very careful when taking a cat from a country home into a city environment: it may be terrified by the noise and thundering traffic, and if it is let out on its own, it will be quite unprepared for the dangers of city life.

For a short visit to a friend's house or to a holiday apartment, a cat can be kept indoors – though you must be careful that no doors or windows are left open through which it can pop out; it surely will, if only from curiosity. Those who insist on their cat accompanying them to a hotel should be warned that the chances of it disappearing are far greater. No matter how careful you are, someone is almost bound to leave a door open, and puss may streak out. However, in a better class of hotel you will at least have the consolation of knowing that it is probably heading straight for the kitchens!

Travelling abroad

If you plan to go abroad for a holiday, far better to leave your cat behind than to subject it to sea or air travel, and if you live in Britain, Hawaii, or any other territory that is free of rabies and has strict quarantine regulations, you will have no choice. To keep out rabies, these countries insist that on entry rabies-prone livestock must go into isolation in specially licensed quarantine areas until they can be declared free of any infection. There are heavy penalties for those who smuggle animals in. This means that a British cat, for example, can be taken freely with you to France or Spain, but on its return would be separated from you for six months – during which time you would not even be allowed to touch it. Any cat would prefer to be parted from you for your holiday rather than for the six months after you come back, and no doubt you would prefer the cost of boarding to the substantial expense of putting it in quarantine.

Those who are going abroad for a long period, perhaps to work, but know they will eventually return to a quarantine country, or are moving to one, will have to weigh up carefully the arguments for and against taking their cat with them. Make sure the pros and cons are considered from a feline point of view and do not just reflect your own convenience.

Quarantine catteries must meet very stringent standards: to prevent the spread of infection, for example, the spaces between pens and between pens and people are strictly controlled by government regulations. Such catteries must also be escape-proof. Each cat is allocated its own, separate quarters and equipment, strict hygiene is observed and staff wear protective clothing which must be changed frequently to prevent any infection spreading from cat to cat or to outside the cattery.

If you visit a cat in quarantine, expect similar rigorous treatment. The isolation principle is relaxed only when cats belonging to the same owner arrive together, in which case they may be allowed to share the same pen.

Cat-sitters and catteries

No cat should ever be left on its own while its keepers are away on a visit, even for a weekend. Arrange for someone to come in to feed and look after it – preferably someone the cat already knows, and certainly someone who will enjoy spending a little time with it. Make sure you leave clear instructions about food and feeding times, together with the vet's telephone number and a note of how you can be contacted.

If you cannot arrange a cat-sitter, then your remaining option is a boarding cattery. At holiday times these establishments tend to be heavily booked, so plan well ahead. Make a scouting mission to the cattery of your choice to ensure that it is clean and well run, with generous ventilated runs for the cats and sufficient space between each run to cut down risks of infection.

Before your cat is accepted at a cattery you will have to produce certificates to prove that it has up-to-date immunization against feline infectious enteritis. Beware of any establishment that does not insist on this precaution: the chances are greatly increased of infection spreading rapidly through all the cats lodged there.

By all means give the cattery instructions on your cat's diet and foibles – but unless it is a diet for medical reasons, do not expect a busy cattery to pay too much attention to them. In any case, a 'holiday' is often a salutory way of teaching a faddy cat to accept a different diet: the owner that it can usually twist round its

claw is not there, and while cattery attendants will care for it with attention, they do not have time to make scores of different meals.

In fact, cats that become accustomed to being boarded when comparatively young may actually enjoy a couple of weeks in different surroundings, with plenty of new felines to make friends with or show off to in the other pens. For them it is like a cat's holiday camp, with their own chalet and attendant staff – but this will not stop them taking it out on the owner who deserted them. Some cats rush to welcome returning owners and the prospect of imminent release from what they consider a ghastly stalag, but most will sniffily refuse to speak. After all, did *they* say that their regular staff could go on holiday? On the other hand, it is not advisable to put an older cat into boarding kennels if it has hardly ever been away from home before; the disruption of its regular routine could be too disturbing.

4. What is a cat?

The cat family's ancestors evolved into a very cat-like form more than forty million years ago – ten million years before the dog appeared, and long before the first human – but the cat was domesticated comparatively late. The dog was hunting with stone-age man, but it was not until the Nile Valley civilization of the pharoahs that the cat moved into human homes. That is quite recent in evolutionary terms, and the cat has not been specially bred, the way dogs have, for particular tasks, so that it is little changed from its wild ancestors. The wild cats of northern Europe look very like modern domestic tabbies, though bigger and heavier, and distinguishable by their larger skull and rather short, bushy and rounded tail.

WILD CAT

DOMESTIC CAT.

The cat's physique

A cat's skeleton is very like our own, except that we have lost all but the vestige of a tail, and the cat walks on the equivalent of our fingers and toes. It can turn its head almost right round to the rear, its limbs are very flexible, and its spine much more pliant than ours. The pelvis and hind-leg muscles are very strong, enabling a cat to leap powerfully, even from a stationary position, and its neck and shoulder muscles help to deliver a killing strike to prey. The main parts of the cat's body are shown in the illustration on page 58.

Watch a cat washing itself and you will see how it can twist its body. The height and length it can jump in proportion to its size amply display its muscle power: just hope that your cat never sinks its teeth into you or strikes out in anger with its rear legs – they can be murderous. Yet that same power can be restrained to give a playful nip of the ankles as part of a game, and the paws can land so softly with the claws carefully withdrawn – and some cats delight in having those powerful paws massaged between the toes and pads.

Its lithe physique makes almost any cat look elegant and beautiful, especially in movement, but this beauty is the visual manifestation of a highly tuned machine designed for finding, hunting, and killing prey.

Because a predator cannot be certain of a regular kill, it has to be able to eat as much as possible of its prey at one sitting and then go without food for several days, if necessary. For this reason the digestive system takes up a large proportion of a cat's insides, and so the heart and lungs are proportionately smaller. This means that the cat cannot sustain energetic activity for long periods. It can run very fast for short bursts, but even at walking pace will tire much more rapidly than a human – even half-an-hour's leisurely walk is likely to prove too much.

Cats tend to alternate energetic periods with long rests, and spend much of their time asleep as even the least observant of owners will know. In more comfortable situations they may sleep very deeply, but more usually, even though they appear lost to the world, their senses are still partially alert for unusual sounds or signs of danger.

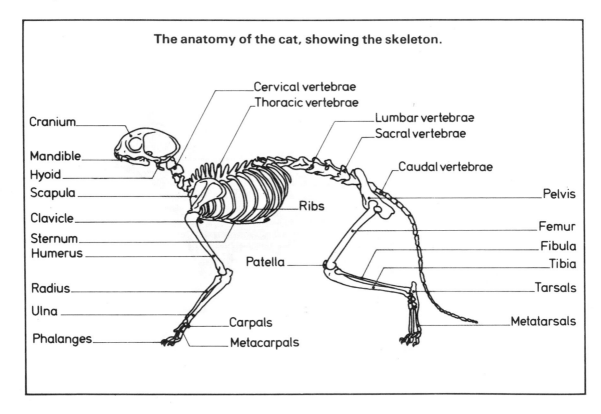

The anatomy of the cat, showing the skeleton.

Cervical vertebrae
Thoracic vertebrae
Lumbar vertebrae
Sacral vertebrae
Caudal vertebrae
Cranium
Mandible
Hyoid
Scapula
Clavicle
Sternum
Humerus
Ribs
Pelvis
Femur
Fibula
Tibia
Patella
Radius
Ulna
Phalanges
Carpals
Metacarpals
Tarsals
Metatarsals

The cat's senses

These are very highly developed and are operational over a much wider range than those of most humans. A cat's perception often seems to be much more acute and its reactions faster than our own. As a nocturnal and twilight hunter, it must be able to see in poor light, hear the slightest noise, and have excellent judgement of distance and space. It appears to be able to remember and identify a wide repertoire of sounds, images, and smells, so that it will recognize your footsteps or your car engine long before you actually reach home, hear the food cupboard opened several gardens away, and know by its scent exactly which feline interloper has crossed its own yard.

Many people think that a cat may even have a sixth sense that most humans have lost, or at least never awaken, but first let us look at those we share.

Sight

Despite popular belief, cats cannot see in the dark – not real pitch dark, though we might find it apparently pitch black when they do not. Vision demands light of some kind and the cat's eyes make the maximum use of whatever light there is. Its iris opens wide to let in as much light as possible, and a reflecting layer at the back of the eye doubles the intensity of the message. In bright light the iris narrows to a slit – if it is still too strong there is an opaque membrane (the nictitating membrane) that can lift from the inner corner of the eye to filter the dazzle.

This extra 'eyelid' also serves to protect the delicate surface of the eye from dust and scratches, as well as helping to clean it. Should the membrane remain up for long periods it is usually a sign of sickness, though it can remain partly up even in some healthy cats.

Cats do not see in such clear colour as we do. Colour is not so apparent in the moon and starlight, or the soft light of dawn and evening when cats are likely to be out hunting in the wild, so they do not need to – although in daylight this means they cannot distinguish shapes as easily as we do. This is why cats frequently do not notice something until it moves; they rely on scent and sound to alert them to concentrate their vision.

Like us they see in depth, but the angle of their eyes allows them to see further behind them, and their flexible necks twist to give an almost total view around without much movement. Cats cannot focus their vision on very close objects. If you bring your hand towards your nose, you will find that it goes out of focus. For the same reason you will often see a cat that has apparently 'lost' a morsel of food right under its nose. Try an experiment: put a small sweet or a piece of biscuit or cheese on the table in front of you, then try to pick it up in your mouth. This is much like a cat's sensation when eating. You may be able to see the food almost to the last moment, when your nose probably gets in the way and your senses of touch and smell take over. Cats do not get quite so close before they need non-visual help, but with them it is probably the nose itself, and their sense of smell, that does the close-range locating.

Smell

The cat's sense of smell is highly developed but does not seem to play a very important role in hunting, although it must help in locating prey. It is used from the moment of birth, whereas the eyes do not open until about the eighth day, and even then are not properly operational. It is scent, not sight, that guides a kitten to its mother's nipples for its first meal, and scent that helps it to locate its mother if it wanders away from her.

As the cat gets older, it uses scent to mark its own territory and to recognize that of others, to identify friends and strangers, to exchange a whole vocabulary of signals about sexual state and readiness, and to find and identify all kinds of objects. Scents seem to give cats an enormous amount of pleasure. A cat will sit and sample the scent messages on the air and savour those it finds of special interest by opening its mouth and drawing air up into a cavity just behind the first incisor teeth, leading to a spiral scent organ called Jacobson's organ. Humans lack this, although other animals have it, and it is to this organ that a snake returns its flickering tongue to 'taste' the scents it picks up on the air. Often a cat will stop breathing to concentrate a smell and then pull a grimace that to you may suggest distaste but is usually exactly the opposite. This behaviour is known as the 'Flehman reaction', from a German word that is inadequately translated as 'grimacing'.

THE FLEHMAN REACTION

A cat's idea of a delightful aroma may not be one you share, and though some perfumier's products seem to please them, most cats are not very fond of the spirit content of synthetic scents, and tend to dislike strong citric smells. Almost all cats like the scent of the plant *Nepeta cataria*, a mint appropriately known as catnip, to which they react by sniffing and biting the plant and rolling about, often over the plant, in a state bordering on ecstasy. It is not only domestic cats that respond to catnip, even full-grown lions have been observed responding in the same way. It has been suggested that the plant's scent is similar to that of a cat's sexual signals, although cats show a similar, but less pronounced, reaction to a variety of other mints. Siamese, on the other hand, do not seem even to respond to *Nepeta cataria*, and yet they are a breed that frequently exhibits marked sexuality. Perhaps the explanation is simply that the chemicals in the plant give the cat a pleasing 'high'.

Sexual signals are carried over long distances by scent, most markedly the indication that a female is ready to mate, for with the onset of readiness her scent becomes distinctly different. This will be recognizable to humans at close quarters if they are very sensitive to smells. No one could fail to notice the reek of feline urine, especially that of toms, when used to mark territory, though it is unlikely that you will be able to identify that of an individual, as cats will do.

In addition to the odours in urine and faeces, a cat has scent glands all over its body, especially around the anus, along the tail, on the lips and chin, and on either side of the forehead. Note the way a cat rubs against a person or an object: first the side of the mouth, then the forehead, then the body and finally a curl of the tail – thus all the main scenting patches are brought in contact.

When you come into the house and your cat runs to greet you, that greeting is also a reinforcement of its claim, laying a scent marking over any marks that may have been placed by others while you were out. But perhaps your cat will be more interested in what you have brought home than in you, and will carefully sniff out everything in your shopping bag to see not only what might be for dinner, but to check for any interesting scent messages from your bag, clothes, or person that show where you have been and whom you have met.

The same behaviour pattern occurs when greeting another cat – a thorough sniff to confirm friendship, a reciprocal marking, and an investigation of odours that is the equivalent of having a friendly chat about what you have been up to.

Hearing

Vocal messages may not be nearly so important to a cat as scent, though the cat has a wide repertoire of sounds ranging from a soft chirrup to a caterwaul. The standard miaow, which everyone thinks of as the basic cat voice, is mainly used in conversation with humans. It is an attention-getter, probably spoken more loudly than a cat would speak to its own kind. Cats, it seems, have realized that humans do not usually notice anything more subtle, and have quite rightly decided on some self-assertion. In fact, most cats develop a polished variety of miaows when specific things are wanted – food, attention, more food, more attention, and so on. Perhaps the basic miaow is a development of the sound a kitten uses to get attention from its mother.

The female has a loud and piercing mating call, often used to effect at two o'clock in the morning under your bedroom window. It is especially excruciating in the Siamese, which often has a rather raucous voice anyway. Like the scent of the female in season, it can carry far – no matter how deep under the bedclothes you may go. Not to be second-bested, males make an equally loud noise that used to be thought an equivalent mating call, but evidence now suggests that groups of cats may actually gather together to 'sing to the moon' in a caterwauling concert that has nothing immediately to do with sexual competition. They usually gather on territory not claimed by any particular cat, so, if your cat is allowed out, they probably won't be in your backyard but plaguing someone else. The male's courtship voice is, by contrast, a soft and seductive cooing sound.

Kittens make a series of squeaks and chirps, and mother cats usually use a chirrupy sound to call their litter. Greetings to other cats (or sometimes humans) are a sort of trilling *prrrrow*, while the continuous, unvoiced purr is the obvious sign of a contented cat – though a deeper one can sometimes be heard when a cat is actually in pain. The deep howl of distress is equally distinctive. Warning yowls, which a cat will expect you to understand, develop into the whole vocabulary of hisses, snarls, shrieks and growls of the fighting cat. A submissive cat seeking to withdraw from a confrontation resorts to the short, quiet sounds of kittenhood.

Many owners come to believe they can understand a great deal of what their cat is 'saying', and will carry on extensive

feline–human conversations – and here those noisy Siamese seem to be among the most talkative. How much sounds convey exact messages and how much is actually being understood through other means is difficult to ascertain. Certainly many owners have trotted obediently to the fridge when 'ordered' to do so by an imperious companion. If you decide that your cat really 'talks', why not document it? You may have a bestseller on your hands.

Cat conversation is probably the least important use to which a cat puts its ears, for they always seem to be on the alert for the slightest sounds. A cat's ears are shaped and ridged for maximum sensitivity, and they can be moved to focus on the sound source. You can see this happening even in an apparently sleeping cat. In fact, cats seem to have more sensitive hearing even than their eyesight, for they can locate the position of the slightest rustle and so know exactly where to find the source of a noise.

At the very lowest frequencies we hear better than the cat, its range beginning at about 30 hertz (cycles per second). Its hearing is roughly the same as ours up to about 2000 hertz, when ours is at its best, about an octave from the top note of a standard piano. Up to 20 000 hertz – around the top note on a violin, which is as high as most humans can hear, and higher than many adults can – the cat's hearing is much better. Its range continues right up to 40 000 hertz before it begins to fade and some cats appear to hear even as high as 60 000. This means that cats can hear many more sounds than humans are able to. We may be fractionally better equipped at the lower end of the range, but cats can hear a whole range of high-pitched noises that we can only register through electronic apparatus. Rodent squeaks that we can barely hear are registered loud and clear by a cat.

Hearing also has a great deal to do with balance, although experiments with deaf cats have shown that they retain the ability to right themselves. The structure of the inner ear, which acts as a kind of balancing monitor, is responsible for warning a cat to twist itself during a fall so that it lands (usually) on its feet. Sight is the other contributor to this ability. Of course, learning to fall correctly is a skill that must be acquired, as anyone who has seen a young kitten falling off something will confirm.

This skill does not mean, unfortunately, that a cat will never injure itself in a fall. There must be time to turn – a fall from a small child's arms, for example, may be too brief to spin the body – while the force of a fall from a height may damage the cat's legs, if they have to sustain too great a shock, or, more frequently, result in an abrupt meeting of jaw and ground.

Touch

If you think of touch you probably think largely of sensation through your fingertips – and a cat's front paws are very touch-sensitive and often used to investigate things – but in fact the whole of the body is sensitive to touch, although many of us only become aware of this when experiencing pain, or the sensual pleasure of a kiss or of silk against the skin. People do not often consciously use the touch-sensitivity of their bodies in day-to-day activities, but unconsciously the body is reacting all the time. Have you ever tried to move about in a pitch-dark room and somehow been able to sense the things around you? Some people are much more sensitive than others to the changes in the pressure of the air caused by close objects, but cats seem to have this sensitivity as part of their basic equipment.

It is probably this, rather than the width of their whiskers (as was once commonly believed), that enables them to judge whether a space is large enough to pass through – but its whiskers are an important part of a cat's sensory system. Together with the eyebrows, the long thick hairs on the back of the forepaws, and lesser pressure spots all over the body, cats' whiskers pass touch and pressure messages to the brain. The tip of the nose is also a very sensitive area.

Cats take great sensual pleasure in being stroked along their back, and some

are located on its tongue. This means that when licking food – and so using the rasp-like surface of the tongue to remove food particles or to pick up liquids – taste messages are immediately received and sensed. The process works in the same way with humans.

But does a cat taste the same things as we do? In fact, experiments suggest that the cat's sense of sweetness is weaker than ours (although kittens have shown a preference for sweetened, rather than plain, liquids), salt is a little stronger, and bitter and sour tastes produce the greatest stimulation. Yet some cats show very clear taste preferences, and sometimes a liking for sweet things such as biscuits: for example, an adult cat that likes to share a breakfast cereal in the morning will indicate quite clearly when the sprinkling of sugar has been forgotten.

The texture of food may also be important, though cats may be perverse. The cat with a liking for breakfast cereal also loves cracking bones, and will grind small ones to powder as though desperate for calcium – yet it completely rejects crunchy, dry cat foods. However, cats should only really be given large bones to chew on; small ones can be dangerous.

also like being stroked or tickled on the belly or a gentle massage between the toes. Touch a cat unexpectedly on the back, even softly, and you will see an immediate ripple down its spine.

Cats seem able to distinguish different textures, and even their thickness, for a cat that digs its claws into a thick sweater as it jumps on to your shoulder will keep them well sheathed if you are wearing only a thin shirt.

Taste

Unlike us, cats do not really hold food in their mouths to enjoy its flavour. Their teeth are designed for gripping and killing prey, and for slicing flesh rather than for mastication, so they cannot chew easily.

As with humans, the cat's taste buds

A sixth and other senses

Do cats have a sixth sense? Many people, and not only apprentice sorcerers and the naturally superstitious, might think it more appropriate to ask which of their other senses to place sixth. But it would be wrong to imply that cats have a sense we lack; it is simply that they make more use of their equipment than most humans do.

For example, cats have a well-developed sense of time. Many always turn up just before you call them for a meal or to come indoors at night, or are even there to meet you when you come back home from work or school. But this is not so surprising: there are many natural signs that help to show the time of day. But a cat that is aware of the day of the week, how is that to be explained? In many cases, your own routine will give the cat the necessary information. A late night followed by a lie-in sets your pattern for Sunday, for example, while the absence of some usual preparation for his or her return indicates this is the day when one of the family stays late to play squash or have a music lesson.

Yet there are plenty of records of cats keeping regular appointments outside their immediate house and family that cannot be linked to established domestic routines, or a change in them. Take the case of Willy (described by Gustave Eckstein in *A Cat that Knows Monday*), who used to stay in on Mondays, instead of departing for his usual evening outing, in order to take an early supper before going off to watch a nearby weekly bingo session through a window. He left home at exactly 7.45 p.m. every Monday evening. Willy could also tell exactly when it was 8.10 in the morning – the time he needed to be home if he was to be let in before his owners went off to work. If he was a few minutes early he could be seen taking his time or even having a pause to lie in the sun, but if he was cutting it fine, he would come rushing back.

The cat of the French writer Alexander Dumas used to accompany him part way to work every morning and then meet him on the way home at the same place. This is not particularly remarkable, but when the front door was opened for him at the usual time each afternoon, the cat would sometimes remain curled up on his cushion, and this proved to be a reliable indication that Dumas would be late! How did he know?

People who are emotionally very close – and, it has been reported, sometimes twins who may not even know the other exists – seem to have an uncanny awareness when something has happened to the other person, even though they may be thousands of miles apart. Most people at some time or other have received a telephone call from someone shortly after having thought of them. A coincidence? Or is there some extrasensory communication involved? There are many stories of cats (dogs show similar

traits) that have seemed to sense some impending danger either for themselves or their owners, or have acted in a disturbed way at a time that was subsequently discovered to be that of their owner's death.

In some parts of the world cats are known to act strangely – miaowing, trembling, and drawing back their ears while their fur becomes erect – shortly before an earthquake. They can probably detect slight tremors unnoticed by humans, but it is difficult to find a similar cause for cats that apparently reacted prior to air raids in wartime, unless they could hear the sound of enemy planes at a great distance and before an air-raid warning sounded. Proverbs from several countries link feline behaviour with weather prediction, perhaps with some plausibility since cats – and many other animals – may be extremely sensitive to changes in air pressure or moisture level.

Much less easy to explain is the ability of cats to find their way home, even from places to which they are taken and have never been before. There are cases of this both when cats have been accidentally taken somewhere – trapped in the back of a van, for example – and when they have been moved to a new home but have subsequently found their way back to their old one. Is it possible they could memorize the route they travelled, even in a closed container they could not see out of? It is unlikely. Or perhaps their sense of direction is attuned to particular or to familiar star positions; we know that migratory birds, for example, can navigate by the sun and stars. But if that explanation sounds far-fetched, what about the cats that have not gone home but *left* it to travel thousands of miles to find their owners? Must we attribute to pure coincidence the documented case where a cat left behind in California turned up fourteen months later in Oklahoma at its old owner's new home? Or the cat that turned up in Texas five months after a family had moved from Louisiana? Or the New York vet's cat that made its way 2300 miles across the continent to turn up five months later in California? A strong homing ability is explicable, but to trace a person over that kind of distance defies explanation. How many other cats go on the same kind of search and fail? Are the successful cats exceptional, or is it the unsuccessful strays that do not match the pattern – or are the strays deliberate adventurers, either looking for something better or simply running from home?

Researchers call this ability to trace a person or another animal into totally unknown territory 'psi-trailing', but they have not been able to explain it. It seems as likely that a cat could read a change-of-address card and a road map as sense where a person has moved to. Perhaps it is not surprising that cats have always been associated with the supernatural.

While some of the cat's abilities are difficult to understand and impossible to explain, there are many aspects of its behaviour that can be interpreted easily by any owner who gets to know their animal. Some will be exclusive to an individual cat–human relationship, and the general patterns are discussed in the next chapter.

5. Feline understanding

The more you know about your cat the better you will be able to look after it, and the more you understand it the more pleasure you will get from the relationship. The last chapter touched on the way in which cats convey messages by voice and scent, but there are other ways in which a cat communicates, and you should learn to recognize them. In recent years we have come to understand much more about human body language, making that of the cat easier to read. By remembering also that the cat is close to its wild cousins, you will find it easier to understand its behaviour.

Creature comforts

Cats are sybaritic creatures. They do not like getting wet, though finding themselves in water most can swim, and the Turkish Cat (see page 129) has a reputation for enjoying a dip. A few drops of water are not likely to do a cat much harm, but a cat finds it very unpleasant, especially if unexpected – which is why the water-pistol or flick-of-water deterrent works (see page 30). However, a few heavy raindrops could be the precursors of a heavy downpour, and a rain-drenched kitten quickly loses body heat and can easily die if left

exposed – so there is an instinct to take cover from water that continues in the adult. If your cat does get soaked in a downpour, throw a towel over it and rub it vigorously dry. When you have absorbed the worst of the wet, brush the fur.

Cats usually do not even like stepping in a puddle, but water is no deterrent when it comes to food. When a cat has discovered how to catch fish, it will certainly not worry about getting a paw wet while flipping a fish out of a pond or stream. Although this is not a skill that many cats master, and the goldfish in your pond are probably more vulnerable to birds than to cats, it may be worth ensuring that the water level is too far below the edge for a cat to dip a paw without

falling in, or fitting a little chicken wire around the edge to keep stray paws out.

Mealtimes

The cat is normally a hunting carnivore, but even wild cats will happily take carrion – such as a rabbit killed on a road – or other food unintentionally provided by man. This means that no cat has to be trained to accept dead meat, which is not the case with some other pets, and fortunately the easy availability of food has a marked effect on a cat's territorial needs, making it less likely to wander.

However, there is no doubt that some cats can be difficult about accepting food if they suspect something tastier might be available. Cats are not unappreciative of their providers – they show them some of the attention that is normal between a kitten and its mother – but, as every cat owner knows, house cats often behave as though things are run exclusively for their own benefit, unless the contrary is made crystal clear. If they have already smelled their favourite food being prepared for the human family, what is the point of spoiling their appetite by eating this rubbish in their bowl? After all, if you were off to a party where you knew there would be smoked salmon, would you fill up beforehand with mousetrap cheddar?

A strict routine, meals at regular times, no feeding at the table, and titbits offered only after your mealtimes and in a bowl may enable you to establish a proper discipline – but do not take risks. If you come in from a shopping expedition, you had better not leave those tempting lamb chops or other goodies unattended while you take off your coat. Either put them safely in the fridge, or keep them beside you.

Safely in the fridge? Even there they may be vulnerable. The intelligent cat will soon cotton on if the door of the fridge can be opened with a hook of the paw, just like any other door in the house.

Is your fridge cat-proof? If it is flush with other kitchen units, then a cat cannot get at the side of it; but if it is not, a paw pushed against the edge of the door from beside the fridge, with claws gaining extra purchase on the rubber seal, will work like a charm. If that does not do the trick, then the 'floor manoeuvre' probably will: flat on the back, paws above the head to grab the bottom of the door, a pull to get it ajar, and then a push with the head to swing it wide open. . . . Luckily, this is a difficult exercise, particularly when the door is a heavy one – but it can be used to great effect on ill-fitting cupboard doors, in order to play a little game, scattering your neatly folded clothes all over the floor.

Knocking over a packet of dry pellet food in order to scoop some out of the top is kitten's play, of course, and so is tearing open thin plastic packs. Cling-film wrapping will not protect those smoked salmon sandwiches you have so carefully laid out, nor the quiches ready on the table for your guests (oh well, no one will know they once had bacon in them, and they will look just about presentable if you cut them into very thin slices).

Threats of enforced detention and short, sharp shocks will not mean a thing, even if the offender is caught in the act. You must accept that when an animal is called an opportunist scavenger it simply means plain thief, no matter how perfectly trained your cat may appear to be – at least, in your presence. Anything you do not want your cat to get at should be kept behind a door that is firmly shut, preferably with a combination lock. You may take great care to see that your cat is adequately fed, but that stolen titbit will always be irresistible. But do not despair. Just occasionally you will have the last laugh: as when one prize thief, having slipped unobtrusively into the dining-room, leapt up onto the table and executed a swift, commando-style raid on his owner's plate, only to realize as he retreated for cover that he had missed the steak and snatched a lettuce leaf instead. And, as you will soon discover, cats do not like being laughed at!

Sleep

Of course, food is not everything. A cat that does not have to go out and hunt for its food will be able to lead an agreeably lazy life. Much of it will be spent asleep, but cats do not pack their sleep all into one long session, as we usually do – they take short catnaps instead. A warm, comfortable place to curl up, a full stomach, and a sense of security will be quite adequate to ensure drowsiness – and so will boredom, especially in a home where the owners are out all day and a cat is locked in on its own. Cats have a simple remedy for inactivity – they sleep through it.

Young kittens and elderly cats both need more sleep than healthy adults. Even within a catnap there are both shallow and deep sleep states. During the former the cat may remain sitting, but in the latter it will usually roll over on to its side and its muscles will relax. In this state it may twitch its whiskers, nose and ears, make a dab with its paws, or even a chattering movement with its mouth (see below) as though dreaming of playing, hunting, or of a delicious dinner – and perhaps it is.

In deep sleep a cat that lives confidently in a secure home can often be picked up by someone whose touch and smell are familiar without waking, though any signal that is associated with danger will bring it to life immediately. Very young kittens up to about four weeks old go almost straight into deep sleep and have no shallow sleep; adults go intermittently from the shallow to deep states.

Temperatures

The traditional image of the cat asleep in front of an open fire is a true one: cats love somewhere warm. Nowadays they will choose the top of a boiler or a radiator shelf in a centrally heated house although the occasional bangs and crashes as the boiler stops may startle even the most lethargic moggie sprawled on top. In a big apartment building with resident cats you may see a number of

them spread out along a corridor. They are not being used as markers by a carpet layer, nor do the distances between them reflect any social hierarchy. They are not even waiting outside their front doors because they have been locked out. In fact, they have simply chosen to occupy the spots where the hot-water pipes or heating elements pass under the floor! Indoors and out a cat will also have its favourite spots for lying in the sun.

Cats are not well provided with sweat glands, and so in hot weather they cannot keep their temperature down by sweating. Instead they will usually take care to find some shade if the weather is very hot, and will certainly avoid unnecessary exertion. A cat shut up in a very hot room – or even worse left in a closed car exposed to hot sun – may soon begin to show signs of heat exhaustion with staring eyes and an open, panting mouth. Emergency action is called for in such an event, to cool the cat down, and veterinary attention will probably be needed as well. See page 119 for more details.

Despite their susceptibility to heatstroke, cats seem able to tolerate much hotter surfaces than we can. True, their normal body temperature is a little higher but, somewhat surprisingly for an animal that is so touch-sensitive, the cat can comfortably walk or lie on surfaces that most humans would find too hot to touch. Cats often lie by a fire roasting themselves until their fur is almost singed, or even let their tail fur frizzle in a gas jet – like a cat that was given to sleeping on a boiler next to a gas hob and only had its tip rescued from more serious harm because the strong smell of singed hair alerted its owner. A cat can tolerate a rise in skin temperature to about 126 °F (52 °C), except on the face, which is much more sensitive to hot and cold.

In cold weather a cat will curl up into a ball and so help to conserve body heat by reducing its surface area exposed to the cold. The hotter the temperature becomes, the more the cat uncurls, so that in strong sunshine or on a very warm surface it may lie with its legs stretched out and its stomach exposed in a long line or even curling slightly backwards. The position allows the maximum amount of heat to radiate from the body.

Territorial imperatives

A cat's sunning spots or favourite indoor resting places are high on the list of those to which it claims an inalienable right. However, with the demands of other cats in a multi-cat household, or of many close neighbours outdoors, it may not be able to establish an exclusive claim and has to accept that its rights are on a time-share basis, valid only at certain hours.

An animal's territorial claims are closely related to its food requirements – the hunter must have a wide enough range to provide it with sufficient prey. Both farm cats and ferals in cities usually need a fairly large territory, although their diet may be topped up with snacks from friendly humans or by scavenging in dustbins. Most domestic cats, however, are not dependent upon the prey

they catch – having to hunt no further than their dish – and so frequently may have a comparatively restricted range. But there is a lower limit to this. Laboratory animals develop neuroses and belligerence when crowded together in too small a space (a condition that may also affect many of us who live in cities), and cats will always try to maintain their distance from one another, much as we do when standing in line waiting for a bus.

However, you will often see cats curled up together. They will almost certainly be cats of the same family, whether actual blood relations, members of a human-centred household, or feral cats belonging to a colony, which are frequently actual close relations.

In very heavily built-up areas such as city centres, free-ranging household cats have to fit in with these feral ranges, although their core area is in the home where they are fed. But pets in the suburbs, where the houses have individual self-contained gardens, tend to share their ranges to a much smaller extent. Indeed, the range may not extend much beyond the garden, with catless household gardens being divided between neighbouring claimants. A newly arrived cat in such circumstances may have some difficulty in establishing its claim to its own backyard, if this has already been parcelled out, unless you give it help by chasing other cats away. A new unneutered tom will almost certainly have to do battle with established toms to decide his place in the local hierarchy, but once that is fixed may not have to battle again unless he later challenges a more dominant cat for its place, is himself challenged, or joins in the fights when another new cat arrives. Cats are not usually active in defence of their whole range, but they will be much more possessive about the more restricted core territory, and even females and neuters will defend it, though some housecats appear to see the dominant humans as doing this for them.

Ranges and territories should not be thought of as concentric areas around a particular spot. They may be most irregular shapes (though frequently making use of the pattern of man-made features, such as walls, paths, hedges and flower beds). They may utilize the top of a wall, or even the branches of a tree, without laying any claim to the areas on either side or below. They may claim their own backyard and that of the catless house next door, and then run across the road to include the front garden of a house several yards down on the other side. Such patterns make use of the spacing, but not the divisions, of human arrangements. On the other hand, family use of an area does appear to have some effect on what a female housecat recognizes as her natural, i.e., family, territory. If you rarely use the front garden except to walk up to the door, then the area might seem more reasonably to belong to the window-cleaner; though if you mow the grass or clip the hedge you have established a claim. Cats do not look at the details of your lease or bill of sale, they follow physical usage.

A cat's territory does not remain constant. Changes in the local cat population will change the pressure on space. An aggressive tom may be allowed much greater intrusion than would be permitted to a female or neuter. Careful and continuous study would be necessary to establish how individual claims operate. It seems likely that a trespassing cat which does not offer any challenge may sometimes be tolerated provided it acknowledges the rightful claimant. When a housecat spends much of its time indoors or is allowed out only at certain times this will affect the pattern. Joint rights of way will be accepted, perhaps right across a territory even though a fringe path is rigorously defended. Remember, therefore, that if you notice a strange-looking man – with camera, binoculars and notebook to hand – surveying your garden you are not necessarily about to be burgled. The visitor may be a scientist engaged upon a study of territorial behaviour in the urban cat

– or so he will say when the police arrive.

Cats of the same household may lay claim to very limited areas, and according to a strict pattern. Two cats, for instance, may both sleep on the owner's bed but one of them claims the right to sole occupancy for the first half hour. Cats may follow a strict timetable for favourite locations.

Free-ranging cats in a neighbourhood frequently share a neutral meeting place outside all individual territories, where they gather at night to socialize. This probably helps to establish a group identity that reduces conflicts. Human parallels are not easy to draw: there are certainly plenty of neutral meeting places in most neighbourhoods – they are called bars – but they do not guarantee a lack of conflict, especially late at night.

Body language

What happens when a cat wants to keep another cat out of its territory, or has to face some other confrontation? Most cats will avoid a fight if possible, though they can inflict a lot of damage if one ensues. But if you watch your cat confront an intruder on the garden wall, it will probably go like this. First one gives a warning, often by means of a low growl; this escalates into a threat display in which both make themselves look and sound as formidable as possible. A cat will show its teeth, hiss, perhaps even open its mouth in a harsh snarl. Its pupils dilate as it fixes the other cat with its stare. Its whiskers bristle and its body hair stands on end as it raises its back, and its ears are pricked to be alert but pinned back against its head so they will be less easy to get hold of if it goes into the attack.

At the opposite extreme is the totally submissive posture in which the cat makes itself as small as possible, crouching low with its head down, ears flattened sideways and whiskers pressed to its face. It may avert its eyes from its opponent and make a plaintive, kitten-like mew.

The arched back stance, which you see so frequently, is actually a combination of reactions of both fear and aggression – the rear of the cat moves forward to attack while the foreparts stay fixed, or even retreat, forcing the body up into an arch. The bristling fur seems to be an instinctive reaction to fear in mammals – even humans feel their body hair, if not their coiffures, tingle as they attempt a threat display at a sudden fright. Sometimes only the tail becomes erect, bushing out like a thick-branched Christmas tree, and it is usually the last section of the fur to go down.

Sometimes a cat will freeze and its fur will stand on end as it appears to watch something you cannot see – for all the world as though it has seen a ghost. The sensation may be strong enough to transfer the tension to humans who are present, and it is not surprising that many people think that cats may have some ability to sense forces in a different dimension from our own.

If the long drawn-out ritual of threat and counter-threat does not produce submission from one party, swipes at the head with the front paws may follow, with claws extended, and attempts to grapple around the neck and bite, which can lead to tight clinches. One cat may risk rolling over on to its back, exposing its vulnerable belly, for this enables it to use the full force of its rear legs to strike out as its opponent comes in to attack.

There is usually lengthy confrontation and manoeuvre between each spurt of action, contact being kept to a minimum. Submission is less effective now; the loser must break away and be chased off by the victor.

In a confrontation with another type of animal, such as a dog, a cat will usually put on a strong threat display, but use it mainly as a way to halt the other's approach while waiting for the best moment to bolt to safety up a tree or on to a wall where it is out of reach. Sometimes the display may be sufficient to make the dog turn tail.

You can see kittens in play go through all these confrontations and fighting patterns, but some inbuilt restraint mechanism keeps their fights within the bounds of play. Their fur protects them from scratches so they rarely cause each other damage. However, even with kittens you may not be immune from sharp teeth and claws if you play fighting games with them – and remember that you lack sufficient fur to offer protection!

With someone whom they have learned to trust, few cats will intentionally inflict injury unless provoked, and they will usually issue plenty of warning that they are getting angry. Learn to recognize the changes in ear position, the soft growls indicating that you have pushed them to the limit. Even if a cat gives you only a warning bite or clawing it can be quite painful – and a serious attack can really wound. However, the more you know your cat and the more it can trust you, the more you will be able to trust it. Cats that have real confidence in their owners may even allow them to inflict pain – as when treating injury – but never take risks, for though your cat may not react as it would to an unknown threat, it will probably still offer resistance. Cats may seem wild and unpredictable and sometimes dash about quite madly, but their feelings and intentions are clearly signalled if you learn to notice.

The first sign of irritation will probably be a lashing of the tail – a useful indicator of a cat's mood. A tail that is carried high, usually with the tip slightly curled, is like a flagpole flying a welcoming banner as a cat approaches you or another cat. This may have some connection with a kitten's behaviour while its mother cleans the anal area, and the

way the tail is held when spraying: both are situations when the cat feels confident and positive. Some cats with very flexible tails will walk with them curled almost level with their back when they are feeling that all is very much all right with the world.

A sleeping, contented cat may move the tip of its tail in a lazy way, but an excited cat's tail will quiver, especially if it is about to leap on something interesting, when the tip twitches though the rest of the body is kept perfectly still. A terrified cat may swing its tail forward between its legs. There is also a scornful and indignant jerk of the upright tail – a feline equivalent to a 'V' sign or a finger to the nose – linked perhaps to the quiver that usually accompanies spraying. It is given, for example, when a cat is called in and does not want to come; and some cats also seem to use it as a gesture of impatience when they are being denied attention, but will not demean themselves actually to ask for it. The tail twitch always suggests some degree of tension, and if it spreads along the length of the tail and the tail begins to lash from side to side this is a sure sign

of irritation, increasing to anger with the extent of the movement. It is a warning that is ignored at your peril.

The tail plays a role in helping the cat to keep its balance, but it can also be very useful for keeping a nose warm in cold weather when curled up for a snooze. A mother's tail (and sometimes that of other cats) becomes a toy for her kittens, and often a substitute prey for teaching them some of the skills of the hunt. A cat's tail always remains its plaything – even the most grown-up cat will still get a great deal of fun from chasing its own tail.

The hunter – in play and for real

Kitten play is a preparation for adult life, for through play the physical skills of hunting and self-defence are acquired. There will be plenty of rough-and-tumble, threat displays, typical aggressive and submissive behaviour, and ambushes and pounces. Attacker and defender will suddenly exchange roles, and there is always an awareness that fighting is 'pretend'. From about one month old you may see your kitten take a strange sideways leap on stiff legs that looks like shocked surprise, but is in fact an effective method of getting out of the way.

There are a number of manoeuvres directly related to catching prey: a forward pounce, which the adult will use for catching mice and similar prey and which you can elicit by trailing a piece of

string; the swat-in-the-air (dangle something on a string for this one), which is useful for striking at a bird; and the scoop-with-the-paw, used to flick a ball of crumpled paper in the air, which could land a fish if timed correctly. Kittens soon learn to dribble like any soccer star.

All kittens will indulge in this 'hunting play', but unless taught to hunt for prey may not grow up to be hunters. Indeed, unless their mother brings them prey, and perhaps later takes them out hunting with her, they may not even link the chase with food. If you want a cat that does *not* hunt, find a female that does not hunt and have one of her kittens almost as soon as it is weaned. If you play with it, the kitten may come to regard its hunting instincts as a normal part of cat–owner activity, rather than using them on furred or feathered visitors to the garden. On the other hand, a cat that is over-socialized when very young may become so fixated on its owner that it is distressed if you are not there, so make sure that it is used to your being away

from time to time. Cats that become over-dependent upon human company sometimes refuse to eat when boarded in a cattery or otherwise 'deserted' by their owners.

The hunting cat can be a very patient animal, waiting for long periods along a route where it expects prey to appear, sitting by a mouse hole or hoping for a bird in range, but more frequently it will locate prey by sight or scent and go after it. Watch a cat stalking in the garden. It moves almost silently through cover, making a dash where there is none and freezing whenever its prey might observe it. It will lower its ears when looking over an obstruction to avoid an obvious silhouette, and keep its stomach low to the ground with the body stretched out to be as unobtrusive as possible, until it has got as close as it can without revealing its purpose.

If close enough, especially from a position higher than the prey, a cat may leap straight on to it. More often, and especially with large prey, it will make a last dash or leap to a spot beside the victim, so that, with its rear legs anchored to the ground, it can strike from a stable position and maintain that stability if there should be a struggle.

The kill is made by a firm bite on the back of the neck that is guided by the break between head and neck, the teeth severing the spinal cord between two neck bones. The whiskers and touch-receptors at the base of the teeth help to locate the exact spot to bite.

If you watch from a window, or at a distance where you will not disturb a cat hunting – remembering that it is not trying to hide from you – you will see all of these actions. When a cat is almost ready to spring it will begin to quiver with excitement. The hind legs may go through treading motions, the rear swing from side to side and the head move to help judge precisely the correct distance, while the tail will almost certainly flicker at the tip even when everything else is poised for action. You may even see a cat go through these manoeuvres when it is watching prey through a window, and you will often see a cat make a machine-gun-like chattering at prey beyond its reach. It sounds like sheer frustration – and probably is exactly that, triggered off because in a less exaggerated form this is the movement used to locate the spot for the neck bite. Since the cat realizes it cannot reach the prey, it is in effect demonstrating what it would do if it could.

Birds, at which this action is most often directed, are usually stalked by the cat dashing from cover to a point where the bird may see it, freezing until something interrupts the bird's line of vision (remember, birds can see behind themselves), and then dashing forward again. Since a mature bird is rarely pounced on before it takes wing, the attack usually consists of a blow to knock the bird to the ground as it becomes airborne.

Large prey such as rats may also be battered initially with the paws before an attempt to kill. This has the effect of subduing the animal's resistance, and is thought to be connected with the way cats sometimes play with their victims before killing them.

A cat should never be punished for bringing its prey home to you. It should be thanked for the present, however much you would like to reject it – though you might try to train your cat not to bring such offerings into the house! If you are unhappy at your cat being a hunter, you should think twice about having a cat at all: cats must eat meat – and even if it is canned, some animal must die to provide it.

6. Some sense about sex

Cats have gained a reputation for excessive sexuality, perhaps from the attention that their mating calls attract, but is this reputation in any way deserved? They do not have the drastic battles over sex that occur with rutting stags, for example, nor do they make the extended public display common with dogs – though I remember one occasion when a female dragged her boyfriend in from the rain and straight under the table in the middle of a dinner party. Have you ever seen a tomcat work off his frustration with another in the street like brazen dogs? The gay tom stays definitely in the closet. A cat may jump on a visitor's lap, but it does not rape her legs!

The female cat has probably been maligned by the sexist attitudes of the past for, though canine, human and all other mammal females advertise their sexual interest by the scents they produce, most men were unaware that they were responding to female odours, or pheromones, until scientists studied the matter. The female cat, on the other hand, does not rely on scent but shouts from the roof-top (or at least the window-ledge) that she is interested in sex, thereby offending the behaviour codes of male-dominated societies. The courtship of the cat, unlike opportunist canine rape, can bring a line of free-ranging toms queuing up outside a calling female's home and, for some, recall attendance at a brothel – so often called a 'cat house'.

Some cats, especially Siamese, at times do appear to be very randy. Domestic cats certainly come into season more frequently than wild ones.

To neuter or not to neuter

A feline pregnancy lasts sixty-four days, give or take a day or two, so it is quite possible for a cat to have three litters, each of perhaps six kittens, in a single year. If about half those kittens are female, then in only four years you could have more than 2000 kittens, grand-kittens and great-grand-kittens. That is a lot of kittens to find homes for!

Although kittens of some pedigree breeds are in great demand and fetch high prices, every year there are many

Pregnant again. Third ruddy time this year!

thousands of kittens for which no homes can be found and that have to be put to sleep, or that are abandoned, probably to die more painfully. Unless you intend to breed, you should have your cat neutered.

Neutering reduces the urge to spend a night on the tiles and may make males less belligerent, but has no harmful effect. Neuters sometimes take less exercise and more easily gain weight if overfed. Do not over-indulge them.

If you keep an 'entire' tom (that is, unneutered) for breeding, you will need to keep it permanently penned or indoors, and an 'entire' female will have to be kept in the house when in season unless you want her to have kittens. If you let her out, there are enough free-ranging toms for her to find a mate – in fact, probably several. If she is a pedigree, you will want to find a suitable stud tom to match her qualities and produce good kittens.

Neutering used to be undertaken when toms were very young, but today it is usually postponed until about six months, when they are nearer puberty. It becomes a slightly more awkward operation but will not have any risk of affecting the cat's development; neutering very young males could affect the size of the urethra and lead to urinary problems when the cats grow old. However, if you wait until a tom reaches full maturity, it may continue to mate, spray territory and fight with other males for some time, and spraying may persist.

Male neutering is usually simple castration. Females are usually spayed, as it is called, in which most of their sex organs are removed. This is a more complicated operation, and consequently more expensive (though think how much feeding all those kittens would cost!), but one that many vets perform several times a day. It is usually carried out before the cat is sexually mature, but can be done after a cat has had a litter. It should not be done when the cat is in season unless for urgent medical reasons.

The operation

Make arrangements with the vet in advance. Castration takes only a few minutes, spaying less than half-an-hour. Today both are performed under general anaesthetic, so the cat should not be fed for twelve hours beforehand, or given water or other fluids for six hours before. Usually the cat will be allowed home the same day and must be kept quiet and indoors for about forty-eight hours.

A female will have a small patch of fur shaved where the incision is made – it will soon grow again – and will have to be taken back about a week later to have her stitches removed. You should not encourage the cat to play energetic games but to rest as much as possible. Keep an eye open for the rare occasion when she might pull out some of her stitches before time. Ring the vet if she does and he will tell you whether to rush her in to him or whether it is really still quite safe.

The queen in season

A breeding female, a 'queen' in cat-fancier's jargon, usually shows a marked change in behaviour when she is coming into season, or oestrus – though one or two learn to suppress the signs, at least when their owners are around, so that they can get out to mate before they are stopped. She will usually make more displays of affection: rubbing against people and things, rolling on the ground and softly miaowing. She may seem generally restless, show less interest in food, and urinate more frequently than usual. She is also producing the pheromones (scent signals) that tell toms she will be interested in mating, which the keen-nosed owner who handles her a lot may also be able to notice, along with a juicy secretion from the vagina.

It is worth learning the signals, for you may find toms lining up outside even before your cat begins to make the characteristic and obvious vocal call, like a baby howling. Try stroking her right down to the base of the tail and she will probably take up a crouching position, sweeping her tail to one side and raising her rump in a position ideal for mating.

The mating

Cat pairings can sometimes seem very romantic affairs – a stud tom and his visiting female curling up to sleep together, playing with and grooming each other between their sexual bouts like a honeymoon couple. Sometimes there may be only the minimum courtship. If a queen is allowed to mate freely, there may be a number of male suitors and fights may break out among them for the right to mate. The female, however, will not necessarily accept the victor. Queens are choosy animals and will reject the advances of a tom they do not like, though they may mate with several suitors. It is possible for a litter to include the kittens of more than one father.

Gestation table. Gestation in the cat lasts an average of 64 days, but may vary by a few days either way. This table is intended to help you work out the date of delivery (the right-hand column) 64 days after mating (the left-hand column). Remember to deduct one day from the expected date of delivery during leap years for matings from 27 December to 28 February.

MATING		DELIVERY		MATING		DELIVERY	
January	1	March	6	July	2	September	4
	8		13		9		11
	15		20		16		18
	22		27		23		25
	29	April	3		30	October	2
February	5		10	August	6		9
	12		17		13		16
	19		24		20		23
	26	May	1		27		30
March	5		8	September	3	November	6
	12		15		10		13
	19		22		17		20
	26		29		24		27
April	2	June	5	October	1	December	4
	9		12		8		11
	16		19		15		18
	23		26		22		25
	30	July	3		29	January	1
May	7		10	November	5		8
	14		17		12		15
	21		24		19		22
	28		31		26		29
June	4	August	7	December	3	February	5
	11		14		10		12
	18		21		17		19
	25		28		24		26
					31	March	5

Pedigree mating

If you want to breed your pedigree female, you must make arrangements with the stud cat's owner well in advance of when you think she will come into season. You will usually have to pay for the liaison, often a hefty amount. As soon as you think she may be coming into season, telephone to make sure your chosen tom does not have another queen booked with him. An unmated female may advertise her needs with persistent 'calling' and be prepared to mate for up to ten days if no male is available, and in fact is usually most receptive towards the end of that period, so you probably have a day or two in hand if the tom is occupied. There is usually a two or three week period between heats if you miss the first cycle.

If your cat does not become pregnant, the tom's owner will probably allow a free mating, but is under no obligation to do so. The owner should, however, have ensured that several matings have taken place before your female is returned to you.

The pregnant cat

If successfully mated, the queen's oestrus lasts for only another three or four days. Make sure she has no access to any other tom during this time or you may find to your dismay that she conceives his kittens as well as, or instead of, the ones you want. Unlike humans, cats ovulate only in response to mating (unlike dogs and humans, they do not menstruate), and fertilization does not actually take place until 24–36 hours after mating. The table on page 81 will help you to calculate the expected date of delivery from the time of the first mating.

The first sign that she is pregnant is when the nipples become pink, erect and a little enlarged. This is more noticeable with a first pregnancy, and becomes apparent about sixteen days after mating. By about the end of the third week an experienced vet can confirm that she is carrying kittens, for he can locate the embryos as pea-sized lumps. Do not try to feel them yourself. It will be another two or even three weeks before the cat's abdomen becomes noticeably distended.

A pregnant cat needs more food. If she is used to having only one meal a day, encourage her to eat breakfast too, for as the pregnancy develops she will find it easier if her stomach does not have to try to deal with all her needs in one go.

How much more food she will need will depend upon how active or inactive she was before, and how big a cat she is – it may be nearly twice as much for a small and normally inactive cat – so if she asks for food you should give it. Mix in vitamin and mineral supplements, but if the cat's physique is such that large kittens could be difficult to deliver, be careful not to overdo food or calcium supplements.

You should also check during pregnancy, and especially towards the end, for any signs of fleas, ear mites or other parasitic infestation. Treat any you do find as soon as possible. Young kittens are very susceptible to such problems, as they are to the insecticides you will use to eliminate them. In fact, the best thing to do is to take the mother to the vet for a complete prenatal check-up.

Preparing for birth

As it gets near the time for her kittens to be born, the mother will try to make a nest in which to give birth – you will notice that she is restless and appears to be exploring odd corners. Keep her indoors, for you do not want her to choose some cold, secluded place. By this time she may also find running and jumping much more awkward.

Ten days or so before the kittens are expected, make up a box about 2 ft (60 cm) square and 20 in (50 cm) deep – or use a cardboard box about that size. Cut an opening on one side at a height at which the mother can easily climb in and out, but not so low that the kittens could crawl over it, and line the box with plenty of newspaper. If it has a top, which will help cut down draughts, it should be removable so you can see inside and help the cat if necessary. Choose a warm place away from bright light and disturbance but easily accessible. Place the cat in the box occasionally to make sure she gets the right idea. She may start to tear the paper up to make a nest – a good sign of approval. If she does not take to the box, note where she seems to favour and move the box there, unless it is plainly unsuitable. If you do not succeed in establishing a kittening place, you may find she decides to have them in an awkward corner of a cupboard, or even on your bed.

If the cat has been used to going outdoors, you must reintroduce her to a litter tray. In the latter stages of pregnancy some cats suffer from constipation. A little uncooked liver in the diet or a spoonful of olive oil or medicinal liquid paraffin (mineral oil, not kerosene) should put that right. If she is producing

a large litter she may also have trouble reaching her rear to wash, so you can gently wash her rear parts with a little warm water. Pat them dry carefully with a cloth. It may also help to trim away some of the genital hair.

Make sure the birth room is warm. Ideally it should be 72°F (22°C) or warmer. In a cold house you could hang an infra-red bulb about 4 ft (120 cm) above the box.

Birth

The signs that birth is imminent may include increased displays of affection, traces of milk on the nipples, and perhaps a slight discharge from the vulva. This discharge may appear a day or two before labour begins and is quite normal, but it should be clear. If it is discoloured or smells foul this could indicate an internal problem and you should contact your vet immediately. The mother may tear up anything to hand – not just the paper in her box – and will probably alternate scratching and squatting. She may even be sick, vomiting her last meal from sheer excitement or simply because she ate it far too quickly, or because her first contractions are beginning. All these signs may be so brief they are unnoticed – or last for as long as a whole day and night. Get in touch with your vet beforehand so you will know where to contact him in the unlikely event of there being problems.

Some cats like to be left on their own when giving birth to their kittens, some like lots of company, some like only their particular human with them; some – mainly Orientals – will even delay giving birth until a particular person gets home. It is probably best to follow the cat's guidance as to whether she likes other cats around as well as humans. Sisters may be welcomed, and even a neutered male has proved an instinctive nurse, washing kittens as they are born.

Your job is to add a towel or blanket to the kittening box and to keep watch if required, or to leave her in peace, especially if she has had a litter before without any problems. If you are going to stay with her and play midwife, give your hands a good scrubbing (but *not* with carbolic soap), and have another clean, rough towel and a wrapped hot-water bottle handy. It is all very exciting, but keep calm: your agitation could upset the cat. She may need reassurance, especially if it is her first litter.

By now she will probably be beginning to pant and will soon start having contractions, which may start at only one an hour but increase to about two per minute. If she is agitated talk calmly to her and gently stroke her belly.

It is easy to miss the dramatic moment when the first kitten appears wrapped in its bubble-like sac, though sometimes it may take the mother some effort to expel it. If the membrane covering the kitten has not already broken, the mother's licking will break the film and clean the kitten, stimulating its breathing; then the cat bites through the umbilical cord. At its other end, though not perhaps expelled until the next contraction, is the placenta, looking like a lump of liver.

You should check that for every kitten a placenta follows (except for twins, which sometimes share one), for if one remains within the mother it could cause post-natal problems. The cat will usually eat the placenta.

While mother deals with the next kitten, sometimes soon after or sometimes after a gap of as long as an hour, the newborn should find its way to her nipples. If it does not, help it. Each individual birth may be rapid, or may take as long as half-an-hour. Only if a kitten is presented rearwards, with one leg and the tail outside and the other leg trapped inside, is there likely to be a problem. If this situation is maintained for longer than half-an-hour you should call the vet. Do not hesitate to contact him or her at any time if you think mother or kittens are in difficulties.

A first-time mother may be uncertain, or perhaps kittens may follow each other too quickly to get proper attention. Then you can help by tearing the amniotic sac with your fingers, vigorously massaging the kitten with the towel to start it breathing, seeing that its mouth and nostrils are clear of fluid, and then severing the umbilical cord. To do this, grip the cord between the fingers and thumb of one hand close to the kitten's body, so that you do not tug on it, and with the other hand about 3 in (7.5 cm) further along press the thumb against the first finger and moving the nail from side to side until the cord parts. If a placenta does not come out completely, ease it out with finger and thumb.

When she has time, mother will take over; meanwhile the newborn kittens will be having their first meal and soon will be asleep. The hot-water bottle will be useful for keeping the kittens warm if there is too much going on for them to be placed immediately by their mother.

Once all the litter has been born – most often four to six, but single kittens are not uncommon and litters of over a dozen have been known – mother will take a rest, but make sure water and food are available for her when she needs them.

If it is a large litter she will not be able to raise them all – numbers are a security against high mortality in the wild. To cope with more than six may weaken both mother and kittens. Ask your vet how many you think she should be allowed to raise. The rest should be painlessly destroyed as soon as possible, unless you are prepared to rear them by hand.

Maternity problems

Most births go smoothly, with mother and kittens knowing exactly what to do. There are a few possible problems, however, and you should know how to spot them.

Placental retention

Occasionally a placenta may be retained within the mother, rather than expelled after the kitten. Unless it is removed, it may decay and infect the uterus. An affected cat will show signs of discomfort, though with all the demands made upon

her by the kittens it may not be easy to recognize any change in her behaviour. Her abdomen will clearly be painful if you handle her, however, and lactation will be impaired. She will probably have a fever and you may notice a brown, viscous discharge from her vagina (although a slight discharge of clean blood from the vagina even for a week or two after kittening is nothing to worry about).

The symptoms of a retained placenta usually appear about three days after giving birth, which is three days too many for your cat and a very good reason for counting the afterbirths during kittening. If you suspect that your cat is suffering from the condition, get it to the vet without delay. Prompt treatment with antibiotics and hormones will usually resolve the problem, although in seriously affected cases a complete hysterectomy may be required. As the cat will hardly be able to discharge her maternal duties at such a time, the burden of raising the litter will fall on you. It is a full-time job.

Metritis and pyometra

Metritis is an inflammation of the uterus which can occur after kittening. Symptoms will appear a few days after birth, with the mother showing little interest in the litter. She will probably be very thirsty and may vomit. Hefty doses of antibiotics are the treatment.

Endometritis is an infection of the lining of the womb. In mild cases the cat may be able to carry her kittens to full term, but the litter will be still-born. The condition may affect a cat's ability to conceive at all or cause the mother to reabsorb the foetuses during pregnancy. Antibiotics can help but are not always effective.

Pyometra is when the womb becomes full of pus, a condition perhaps more likely when something has gone wrong during pregnancy and the litter is stillborn. Mild cases can be treated, but the condition is potentially a killer and may require an ovariohysterectomy.

If something goes wrong during the development of a foetus, or perhaps because a cat is carrying too many kittens, the mother may actually reabsorb a foetus into her own body. You will notice this as a heavily pregnant cat going slowly into reverse, so to speak, although it will be harder to spot if the end result is simply that the litter is smaller than usual. Reabsorption, however, can take place only before the skeleton of the foetus has developed and hardened, with the result that just occasionally masses of half-formed tissue may be born along with normal kittens.

Milk fever

This uncommon condition is also known as eclampsia or lactation tetany, just to impress you with a little jargon. It usually affects a small cat that is nursing a large litter and erupts two or more weeks after birth, although symptoms can appear a day or two after kittening or even during pregnancy. The mother will become very nervous and breathe abnormally fast. Her pupils will dilate, there may be muscular tremors and difficulty in walking, eventually leading to coma and death. The condition is thought to be caused by insufficient calcium in the diet and initial treatment takes the form of intravenous injections of the mineral, followed by calcium supplements. Milk fever is fast-acting and potentially fatal, so watch for any signs of it during the critical phases of pregnancy and raising the litter.

Mastitis

Mastitis is an infection of the milk glands, which may become painful and even discharge pus. In consequence, the mother will reject her kittens when they try to suckle. In mild cases, where just one nipple is affected, it may be possible to clear the blockage by gently squeezing – but prompt veterinary treatment is most important. The kittens may become ill from the mother's infected milk and the mother herself will be in no condition to care for them. Antibiotics will usually deal with the problem, but in the meantime the kittens may have to be removed from mother and reared by hand.

Hand-rearing kittens

In the rare cases where a cat proves a bad mother or falls unwell, or accident orphans the kittens, they must be fostered or hand-reared to survive. Handrearing, or partial hand-rearing, may also help if a cat has more kittens than she can really cope with, or if a weak kitten is excluded by its siblings.

Fostering is best, but a lactating female is required that can handle an extra kitten. Rubbing the kitten with a little milk squeezed from the foster mother's nipples makes it more likely to be accepted. Sometimes another type of small mammal that has recently given birth will accept a kitten and feed it together with its own offspring.

Hand-rearing is difficult, arduous and often sadly unsuccessful. You will not only have to take over the role of maternal milkbar, you will also have to keep the kittens clean and make sure they evacuate, then later become responsible for their training. It can be a full-time job. Think twice before you undertake it.

For hand-rearing, kittens must be kept warm: 90 °F (32 °C) the first day and 85 °F (29 °C) for the next week or more, after which the temperature can be allowed to fall to about 70 °F (21 °C). If you suspend an infra-red bulb over a kittening box you can regulate the heat by the height of the bulb.

You will need special kitten-formula powdered milk, which closely matches that of cats. Cows' milk is not suitable for small kittens. Unsweetened evaporated milk (*not* condensed milk) will be the best in an emergency. If you have to feed kittens straight from birth, ask your vet for help as the kittens will not have received the antibodies from their mother's first milk, called colostrum, which gives some protection against common diseases.

Pet stores sometimes have feeding bottles designed specially for kittens, or a doll's bottle (if it has a proper working teat) will do as a substitute. A dropper of the kind used for eyedrops or a syringe can also be used, but are more difficult because if you squeeze the bulb inadvertently and force milk into the kitten's mouth you may choke it – the kitten must suck the milk out in its own time. Milk should be served at about 100 °F (38 °C).

Sit down with a coarse towel on your lap – it will keep you clean and give the kitten something to grip. You can support the kitten against your palm, holding the head between finger and thumb and offering the milk with the other hand. If the kitten shows no interest, try dabbing a little formula on its nose. If it gulps too much and chokes, lift its rear end rapidly to bring up any air. Kittens may need burping just like human babies, but you should not pat them on their back; instead massage their chest and belly.

Rearing the litter

At first your job will be to see that mother is fed and provided for – she will need even more food and milk now that she has to feed the litter – and to make sure that the kittens do not wander into danger. If you cannot give a room over to the family, pen the cats in (a baby-pen works well if it is stable and the sides are not open enough for kittens to climb through).

Kittens cannot see at birth. They open their eyes at about five to ten days, but for three days or so they may produce a gummy discharge that should be cleaned away. They should not become resealed. At about eighteen days they will be crawling around, and at three weeks should begin to stand and to show their first tiny teeth. This is when weaning first begins. You need to provide suitable food for the kittens. First offer a milk-based food (kitten milk or evaporated milk), then add baby cereal, meat-based, strained baby foods and, from about five weeks, gradually introduce a little steamed fish or scraped raw beef. (Baby foods should be served at twice the concentration recommended for humans to suit small feline stomachs.) When completely weaned the kittens will need frequent feeding – five small meals a day – for their stomachs are only about the size of a walnut.

Mother will keep kittens clean, and at the same time massage them with her tongue to stimulate digestion and expulsion of waste, which she will also clean up when they are young. (If hand-rearing you will have to do both, using a rough cloth wrung out in warm water.) Later she will introduce them to the litter tray.

She will keep a watchful eye and if she senses any danger may carry them in her mouth to a place she considers safer. In her haste an inexperienced mother may grab the kittens by any part of the body, but usually she grips the scruff of the kitten's neck between her teeth. This gives her a secure hold, does not damage the kitten and has the effect of immobilizing it. The kitten usually offers no resistance; indeed, it may curl its body slightly, to make it easier to lift off the ground. Despite the weight in her mouth a mother will run at a fair pace, negotiate steps and even jump up and down from walls or leap over obstacles, apparently without worrying too much about the effect on the kitten. The limp state of the kitten probably makes it less prone to injury.

Most cat mothers are extremely patient, playing with their kittens and eventually taking them out on hunting expeditions if they are hunters themselves. However, for even the most dutiful mother there comes a point when she has had enough of sharp teeth tugging at her nipples and continual pestering, and the time she devotes to the litter will become less and less.

From about four weeks kittens can be accustomed to human handling and games and, for long-haired cats especially, gentle grooming sessions should take place every couple of days (see page 49) – not because mother does not look after the kittens, but because they must get used to being groomed by a human.

Finding new homes

This is very much your problem and *not* the mother's. Between about seven and ten weeks, she will become increasingly bored with her litter, though still protective if she senses danger. She will probably not show a great deal of concern when her grown kittens move to new homes – her owner will probably find it much more traumatic after the weeks of raising them.

Finding good homes can be a problem. However much your friends may love the kittens, they may not feel like taking on the responsibility they involve – and you should not press them, for you want your kittens to be well and willingly looked after. If you end up with another half-dozen members of your own household, you should have thought of that before allowing your cat to breed.

Do not expect to make money out of breeding kittens – you would have to be very organized indeed to make a business of it – but even if you are prepared to give your kittens away, it is better not to. Ask for a small payment to be given, if you like, to one of the animal welfare organizations. Paying for something makes most people place more value on it.

Explain all you can about care and about the kitten's routine and give the new owner a diet sheet. Finally, offer to have the kitten back if it is returned within a week; you may save it from being abandoned.

If the pregnancy was an accident and you have little hope of placing a whole litter of kittens, then cull some of them soon after birth and before mother has become aware of the size of the litter. Do *not* drown kittens. They should be properly disposed of by a vet.

7. Practical health care

Most cats, like most people, are basically healthy provided they have sufficient to eat of a properly balanced diet and are not subjected to physical or psychological stress. However, it is as well to accept that even the most carefully maintained individual is likely to break down from time to time, although we hope in a minor way. The elderly cat, of course, will be more prone to certain conditions and the general running down that inevitably accompanies old age – but, once again, understanding on your part will enable you to take better care of a feline senior citizen's more delicate constitution.

Signs of health

A healthy cat is an alert cat that takes an interest in the world around it. This does not necessarily mean that it is always rushing around insisting on being involved in whatever is going on. Some cats, especially the Siamese and other Orientals, do poke their nose into almost everything, but less outgoing cats may simply keep an eye on things from the warmest and most comfortable place in the home. A fit cat will be interested in mealtimes and will keep its coat clean (except for those few lazy young cats that take advantage of a mother or sibling prepared to wash it for them). The fur will have a sheen and will feel good to touch and the cat will have a fresh and pleasant smell. Its eyes will be bright, its teeth white and it will move with a smooth rippling action.

Signs of ill health

The more you know about your cat's habits and behaviour the more likely you are to notice when something is amiss. The change may sometimes be sudden: unless you are unusually unobservant you are hardly likely *not* to notice when the cat is dragging a lifeless limb or being sick all over your most expensive carpet. Other changes may be progressive: a decline in liveliness, for example, or the development of a swelling. You cannot expect to keep your cat under observation for every minute of the day – the cat may anyway come to regard you as Big Brother were you to try – but you should get into the habit of looking at your pet quite objectively when it moves, when it uses the litter tray and even when it is asleep.

Do not let concern for your cat's well-being lead you to the point of hypochondria. The occasional bout of scratching does not necessarily mean that the cat has fleas; like you, it may simply have an itch. Nor is every sneeze an indication of flu or worse: cats react to dust and other irritants just as we do. In any case, think of the cost of rushing down to the vet every time something is even slightly amiss! It is really a matter of common

sense. If you know your cat you are more likely to know whether something is an isolated, trivial occurrence or an indication of a serious condition.

Not all changes in behaviour will be due to disease. Stress caused by the absence of an owner or by disruption to the household may lead to unusual or erratic behaviour. Such stress in itself can make an animal more susceptible to infection, so do ensure that puss is allowed at least one haven of peace and privacy in the home. Those who have boisterous young children will understand the problem entirely.

There are many signs a trained veterinarian will look for that may not be apparent to an owner, but the following are possible symptoms that are both easily noticed and warrant further investigation:

Listlessness
Loss of appetite
Refusal to drink

Excessive drinking
Sitting over a water bowl without
  attempting to drink
Vomiting
Continued dribbling (but cats often
  dribble when happily being petted)
Continual coughing
Bad breath
Yellow teeth
Yellow gums
Inflamed gums
Reddened tongue tip
Ulceration of tongue, gums or palate
Rigid mouth (especially with
  hawking)
Runny nose
Runny eyes
Dull-looking eyes
Raised nictitating membrane
Head shaking
Weaving head from side to side
Gummy discharge in ears
Excessive ear scratching
Excessive scratching anywhere
Repeated licking of the same spot
Weaving body from side to side
Limping
Holding up a limb
Reaction to touch as though in pain
Fur loss
Very dry fur
Diarrhoea
Straining to urinate
Straining to defecate
Blood in the faeces
Rice-like objects around the anus
Discharges from the vagina
Bloodstained urine
Dragging bottom along ground
Swellings or lumps under the skin
Black specks in fur

False alarms

Like us, cats have the occasional off day, even brainstorm in the case of a highly strung individual. It is quite understandable that the inexperienced owner should become extremely worried when, for example, the cat appears to be choking, with its mouth open and tongue jerking forwards with an ugly, gasping rasp. It is unlikely to be attempting an impersonation of Count Dracula; at any rate, this is the time to investigate calmly, not to panic. Perhaps there is an obstruction, a bone wedged in the throat or on the teeth? If so, the cat is likely to be shaking its head in an attempt to dislodge it. On the other hand, it may simply be a hair tickling the back of the throat, especially if the cat is holding its head up. In that case, gently stroke the throat downwards. If the head is down the cat may be trying to be sick, perhaps to regurgitate a ball of fur ingested when washing its coat.

The cat, not you, is the most reliable guide to whether something is seriously wrong. If puss shows signs of panic (and a cat with a foreign body lodged in mouth or throat will rarely act calmly), then you should be prepared for rapid action. And if it is just a false alarm, do not simply breathe a sigh of relief and forget about

Opposite: *The British Blue is gentle, affectionate and shrewd – like its ideal owner.*

Left: *Don't underestimate a determined cat. If you don't want a calling queen to make a break for it, make sure you firmly close all doors and windows. This one has climbed the edges of the glass louvres and pushed the top one wide enough to effect her escape!*

Below: *On the prowl. Cats are superbly skilled hunters and will wait patiently until an unwary victim comes within range.*

Opposite: *Hoopla! Cats are champions at the high jump and long jump. No garden fence is going to keep them in — or out.*

the matter; keep the incident in mind so that you will know what to do should it happen again.

Temperature, pulse and respiration

In a cat these are not at the same levels as they are in humans. A cat's normal temperature is 100–102 °F (38–39 °C), rather higher than ours. Remember that if a cat's fur feels hot this does not necessarily mean that its body temperature is abnormally high. It may simply have been lying in the sun or on a boiler.

A cat's pulse rate will depend upon how excited or nervous it is. If you have just been chasing it, for example, the pulse will probably be racing, as will the rate of respiration. The normal resting pulse rate can be anywhere between 100 and 140 beats per minute. Vets can tell more from the character of the pulse than from its rate, although it is usually faster in the case of fever, pneumonia, poisoning and bleeding, and sometimes slower with some heart conditions and tumours and with debility and old age.

Cats breathe twice to four times as fast as humans and with a burst of activity will soon get out of breath. At rest they will breathe twenty-six or more times per minute compared with only about twelve times for humans and the rate will be much faster with exertion.

Diseases

Cats can suffer from many of the ailments that affect humans – cancer, leukaemia, pneumonia, arthritis, diabetes and tuberculosis among them – but fortunately there are few diseases of cats that can be transmitted to man. However, there are some parasites that can affect both. Cat fleas are different from ours and are host-specific, though they can be a considerable irritant before they realize that they have leaped on to the wrong species and find another cat to jump on.

Scratches from cats can sometimes lead to cat-scratch fever (possibly caused by a virus) which makes the patient weak and can cause the lymph glands to swell. Needless to say, any sign of this should warrant immediate consultation with your doctor and then with the vet.

A potentially more serious problem is the roundworm *Toxocara cati* (see page 109). Its eggs are passed out in faeces and there is a slight chance of picking them up from infected ground. Again, young children are the most at risk of doing so. If infected eggs are eaten they can hatch into larvae inside the body, although only under special conditions. The larvae do not complete their life cycle in man, but travel round the body before dying where they come to rest. In the vast

Opposite: A comfortable niche from which to look down on the world. Cats like a vantage point which allows them to keep an eye on things.

majority of cases they end up in innocuous places, but just occasionally they can get into the retina of the eye or into the brain and cause serious damage. The risk is very slight, but it is a good reason for cat owners to be scrupulous in their pet's toilet-training and to keep open areas, especially where children play, free from feline excrement.

If a cat is allowed to range free there is little you can do to prevent it from coming into contact with other cats which may carry infections or parasites. Look on the bright side: exposure to minor diseases usually helps to build up resistance to them. A house-bound cat is less exposed to infection, although germs can still be carried on the air or brought into the house by other means. If the cat has led a fairly isolated life its resistance to infection may be weak and so it will be vulnerable to any germs that it does pick up. What *you* can do is ensure that your pet is properly vaccinated against the most dangerous of cat diseases and that its booster injections are kept regularly up to date, especially if it has had little natural exposure to disease.

The more common and/or serious feline diseases are dealt with below.

Feline infectious enteritis

This viral disease is one of the most dangerous of all. It is highly contagious, a killer that can develop so quickly that a cat may be dead before any of the symptoms have been noticed. Kittens are particularly susceptible and the virus can also kill the unborn foetus. Fortunately, vaccines now give protection. The first injection can be given at six weeks, provided the kitten is healthy, but eight weeks is the more usual time as otherwise a greater number of booster injections will be needed. Depending on the type of vaccine used, either a single injection is given or two spaced a fortnight apart. Regular booster injections must also be given; a cat entering a show or being boarded should have one at least a fortnight beforehand. It should hardly be necessary to say, of course, that if a newly acquired kitten does not come with a certificate to show that it has been vaccinated already, you should make this a priority with the vet.

Feline infectious enteritis (FIE), or panleucopenia as it is also known, is a disease of the digestive tract that can take as little as two days to develop or as long as ten. You may suddenly notice that the cat is listless and depressed, sitting hunched up, taking no interest in anything and moving off to somewhere less accessible if you try to handle it. The cat will lose its appetite, develops a high temperature and will usually vomit a yellow-stained and frothy liquid, followed by diarrhoea, which leads to dehydration. The cat may crouch by its water bowl, though without drinking, in a hunched position that displays its pain. If FIE is diagnosed soon enough treatment may be effective. The dehydration has to be combated, usually by fluid injections; antibiotics guard against the development of secondary infections and a serum may be given to provide antibodies to the virus. The cat must be strictly isolated and carefully nursed. Even then the chances for a cat that has not been vaccinated are very slim, and if a cat does recover the damage to the gut (which causes the diarrhoea) may prove permanent, leaving this as a recurrent disorder whenever there is a strain on the digestive system.

In any case of suspected FIE, ring the vet *before* going to the surgery.

Cat flu

FIE is sometimes known as cat flu, but this usually refers to two forms of viral infection of the respiratory system – medically known as feline viral rhinotracheitis (FVR) and feline calcivirus infection (FCV). Vaccines are available and offer some protection, but even vaccinated cats may sometimes develop these infections, though they have more hope of fighting them. Symptoms are depressed behaviour and loss of appetite, followed by sneezing, which also spreads the germs. There is usually a yellowish discharge from the nose and eyes as the disease develops; there may be vomiting as well as snuffles and dribbling; there will be a high temperature, and there may be ulceration of the mouth and tongue. Secondary bacterial infections produce complications, though these can be treated with antibiotics. If a cat survives the first couple of days, careful nursing will usually pull it through, but cats can go on excreting the virus for almost a year – continuously with FCV, intermittently, but especially if under stress, with FVR – so care must be taken to keep the infected cat away from other cats and places they might go to avoid the risk of passing on the virus.

Other respiratory problems

A bacterial infection, often subsequent to FVR or FCV, can produce snuffles and sneezes, sometimes with a nasal discharge, conjunctivitis and an inflammation of the sinus cavities. Antibiotics usually succeed in combating the infection but it may recur as soon as treatment stops. Foreign bodies wedged in the nasal cavities, growths and a fungal infection can all have similar effects. Infections of the upper respiratory system can also leave a residue of bronchitis, inflammation of the air tubes in the lungs, but this may result from inhaling dust or substances to which the cat is allergic, or from bacterial infection.

Pneumonia can be an extension of cat flu or caused by parasites, bacteria or fungus, or be the result of food or fluid entering the lungs. Fever, loss of appetite, dehydration, coughing and sneezing may all be symptoms and breathing difficulty will be noticeable. Careful observation will show that the cat is breathing from its abdomen rather than using its chest muscles. Antibiotics to fight infection, sometimes a supply of oxygen, and always rest and careful nursing are the treatment. The condition may be critical for about a week but nursing goes on for at least a month lest the condition recur.

Cats can also suffer from asthma, tuberculosis, pleurisy and lung disorders caused by internal injury or tumours.

Leukaemia

Feline leukaemia (FeLV), a blood cancer

that also produces tumours, is carried in the blood, saliva and urine. It can be passed on by a mother to her kittens, and most easily among cats in close quarters, such as a cattery, but fortunately it does not survive for more than three days outside the body. About two-thirds of cats overcome the infection, which produces weight loss and debility, but symptoms vary depending upon the organs it attacks. Vaccines in production are not yet entirely satisfactory, and cats suffering from the disease are a source of infection to others and should therefore be put to sleep.

Rabies

Rabies is dangerous and untreatable in cats. Britain, Australia, New Zealand and Hawaii have strict quarantine regulations to keep them rabies free, their island status preventing contact with rabid wild animals. In those territories you are not likely to encounter rabies but everyone should know about it, if only to make them take its containment seriously. Smuggling in a cat disguised as a fur collar, or slipping it ashore on a lonely beach, may sound romantic but would be an irresponsible action that could endanger the lives of people and livestock throughout the country. Legal penalties are severe and the destruction of the introduced animal is one of them. In countries where rabies is endemic cats should be vaccinated to give protection against it. In Britain, and some other places that are free of rabies, animals must *not* be vaccinated (except when being exported or in quarantine) lest it

make actual cases more difficult to identify if they occur.

Rabies is transmitted when a bite or recent wound is infected with virus from a rabid animal's saliva. It is transmittable before the animal shows symptoms of disease; for this reason anyone who has been in contact with a rabid animal *must* see a doctor, and any wounds must be washed out immediately, preferably with ethanol, followed by application of tincture of iodine.

The disease has two stages. It first shows itself as a change in character, usually increasing restlessness and a dislike of light and sudden noises. In the second stage the victim becomes very aggressive, and excessive drooling and a change in voice may also be noticed. Cats do not show the fear of water –

hydrophobia – that is a symptom of the disease in humans. It can take as long as six months for rabies to produce noticeable symptoms – which is why that length of time is required for quarantine.

Feline infectious peritonitis

This is another disease caused by a virus. Feline infectious peritonitis (FIP) may attack many parts of the body, including the liver, kidneys, eyes, nervous system and chest, but an inflammation of the membrane lining the abdomen (the peritoneum) is a common result. The cat loses its appetite, develops a fever and produces fluid in the affected area, yellow and sticky in texture so that it may become difficult to drain. Vomiting, diarrhoea and jaundice may also occur. Symptoms may take weeks or even months to appear but infection is rapidly and easily spread, though fortunately the virus cannot live for long away from a host and is killed by disinfection. Cats which develop symptoms have almost no chance of survival. Although the sick cat can be treated to reduce its pain it will not be likely to survive for more than a few weeks and must be isolated or destroyed to prevent the spread of infection.

Nephritis

Kidney damage, reducing the cat's ability to eliminate wastes, may have several causes, including bacterial infection, but a chronic nephritis of unknown cause is most common, especially in elderly cats. It usually develops over a long period so that symptoms may not be noticed until the ailment is well advanced, with the kidneys becoming scarred and smaller. Cats may lose appetite and drink noticeably more water; they will therefore urinate more frequently and may show signs of pain, arching the back when doing so. Sometimes there will be vomiting or diarrhoea, yellowing of the gums and ulcers in the mouth, and the breath may become increasingly unpleasant; the cat itself may begin to develop a urine-like smell. Blood and urine samples will confirm a diagnosis. Treatment may include a special diet and measures to reduce strain in the cat's life to improve its general condition and slow down the development of the disease, but a complete cure is impossible.

Hepatitis

Liver damage in cats is usually caused by poisoning or is a symptom of other diseases. The most distinctive symptom, as in humans, will be a yellowing of the skin, especially of the whites of the eyes and the inside of the mouth, but general loss of weight and appetite will also occur, perhaps with diarrhoea or constipation. Liver damage of any kind is always a serious matter, sometimes fatal, and warrants immediate consultation with the vet if you suspect it.

Cystitis

This simply means inflammation of the bladder. If you see a cat (male or female) straining to urinate, perhaps even squealing with pain, but passing only a little or no liquid, which may be blood-stained and smell very strongly, this is probably the cause. The cat will often appear very thirsty. If the bladder can be felt as a hard round shape, the diagnosis is almost certain – but you must *not* squeeze the bladder lest it burst. Veterinary attention is essential. Cystitis can be caused by bacterial infection or by the development of bladder stones, especially in unneutered females, but the more frequent cause, especially in males, is feline urological syndrome (FUS) in which the urethra becomes blocked with a gritty paste. Antibiotics, in case of infection, increased fluid intake and treatment to make the urine more acidic to dissolve and flush out the blockage may all be used and in some cases a plastic tube will be inserted to enable the cat to urinate. This is a condition which tends to recur so cats prone to it must have their fluid intake and diet watched. Too much dried food and too little exercise help to lead to this condition.

Heart and blood diseases

Heart problems are not frequent in cats. Whereas one in ten dogs may have some sort of heart condition only about one in a hundred cats has anything wrong. Failure of the heart muscle is the most common feline heart disease; strokes and clogged arteries are rare. Blood clots can occur, but instead of causing a heart attack (coronary thrombosis) as they usually do in man they may break up into fragments and most frequently lodge in the aorta, where the blood supply divides to feed the hind legs. If this happens a cat will quite suddenly lose the use of its hind legs because the blood supply has been almost or completely cut off. The legs will feel cold to the touch and have little or no perceptible pulse. Immediate treatment is essential.

Anaemia, the reduction of red cells in the blood, can be caused by vitamin deficiencies, kidney disease or parasites. An anaemic cat's mucous membranes in the mouth and eyelids will become pale and the animal appears generally lethargic. One kind of parasite causes feline infectious anaemia, although no one yet knows how it is transmitted and it has no apparent effect on some cats, unless they are under stress. The condition can be confirmed only by blood tests and requires a long course of treatment with antibiotics. Sometimes it is associated with feline leukaemia (see page 99) and then success is much less certain.

Mouth and teeth disorders

Disorders of the mouth are often symptoms of other diseases, such as nephritis or feline calcivirus, or may be caused by dental problems. Gingivitis, an inflammation of the gums, may first appear as a fine red line where the gums meet the teeth, though it can affect the whole gum until there is bacterial infection and the gum disease pyorrhoea, with a discharge of pus, or a condition in which the gum grows uncontrollably in an attempt to cover the unhealed areas. Gingivitis may be set off by something wedged in the teeth but is often caused by a build-up of plaque and later of hard tartar. This is not usually present in young cats but is common in older ones and should be checked when grooming. The soft white plaque can be removed with a brush (if the cat permits it) or carefully scraped off. If it hardens into tartar it may need chipping off and older cats may need regular descaling under anaesthetic. If the plaque is not removed and leads to pyorrhoea the cat may lose its teeth or, at least, some of them.

A cat with tooth problems will probably claw or paw at the affected tooth or even rub its face against the ground. Fillings are not practical, so a bad tooth has to come out – and if it is one of the big premolars that is a major operation. They are very deeply rooted and your vet will want to follow up with several shots of antibiotic to ensure that no infection develops. The best way to help your cat keep its teeth is to avoid soft mushy food, provide meat that really has to be chewed and hard biscuits if it will eat them, then keep an eye open for any build-up of plaque and tartar. Cats sometimes even clean their own teeth, like one that started off by stealing socks, perhaps as some sort of game, but now takes one to her food bowl and chews on it apparently to clear canned food from her teeth. She swallows the occasional thread that has to pass through her digestive system, but her sock does seem to work as an effective toothbrush.

Eye problems

Runny eyes can have many causes. There are the respiratory viruses; there may be irritation from dust or other particles; or there may be a blockage in the ducts that drain the eye into the nasal cavity.

Conjunctivitis is a condition in which watering of the eyes is accompanied by inflammation of the delicate membrane that protects the outside of the eyeball and lines the eyelids. The membrane becomes reddened and puffy, and the watering may develop into a thick, mucous discharge. Conjunctivitis may be the result of an allergy or caused by soap, fumes, aerosols and other irritants. In serious cases the cornea may become clouded, with pus developing behind it.

Bacterial infections of the eyes are treated with antibiotics. Great care is required in the diagnosis and treatment of a condition in order to prevent any permanent damage and infected eyes should be seen by the vet at the earliest opportunity. Do not simply apply an eye ointment and hope for the best; the ointment may be designed for a quite different infection and in any case can easily become contaminated.

Glaucoma can be a problem in a few cats. It is an increase in the pressure of the fluid within the eyeball, usually caused by dislocation of the lens. The pupil does not react to light and the cornea often becomes opaque. Cataracts are not as common in elderly cats as they are in dogs and humans, but they can occur at any age, making the affected eye look like a clouded glass ball. One cause is a form of diabetes. Surgery can remove the clouded parts, restoring vision to nearly normal.

Foreign bodies in the eye are usually washed out naturally by tears. In obstinate cases you can help by bathing the affected eye in a solution made up of a teaspoonful of salt to a pint (half a litre) of boiling water, allowed to cool of course. If there is no improvement then consult the vet; some objects such as grass awns can become lodged behind the nictitating membrane (haw) and an anaesthetic may be necessary before they can be removed. A nictitating membrane that remains raised is usually, though not always, a sign that something is wrong. It could indicate anything from exhaustion to worms, a nutritional deficiency or worse, and demands a visit to the vet if the problem persists.

Kittens do not open their eyes until they are about ten days old. If the eyes are not open by the twelfth day ask the vet to check them, especially if the eyes appear glued together by any kind of encrustation or there is a discharge. In the latter case have the mother checked too, as the problem could be the result of an infection caught from her.

Ear troubles

Ear problems are mainly caused by parasites (see page 108) or by a grass seed or other foreign body becoming lodged in the ear canal. Tumours and fungal or bacterial infections can also cause trouble. Any kind of head shaking or excessive scratching suggest investigation. If scratching is allowed to continue it may give rise to a large blood blister, known as a haematoma, which needs to be drained and then stitched by a vet. The most common external problem with ears is damage caused by fights, a condition not so much with symptoms as with after-effects. In serious cases, of course, a trip to the vet is clearly in order, perhaps several in the case of a determined feline pugilist.

Bowel disorders

Loose bowels or constipation are more a cause of irritation than a matter of serious concern. They are symptomatic of a number of diseases, but they are much more often just a minor digestive upset resulting from a change of diet or unwise indulgence. Do not ignore them, however.

Constipation does not develop suddenly. If your pet was perfectly all right first thing in the morning but is straining to defecate by lunchtime then constipation is unlikely to be the cause; it takes several days to develop. The condition is sometimes the result of a lack of exercise (especially with cats that are suddenly confined after being allowed to range freely), sometimes because the diet is too dry and occasionally, and simply, because the cat is lazy and overfed. A day without food, but with lots of water and a tablespoon of liquid paraffin or olive oil (no, not castor oil) will probably do the trick. Be sparing with the laxative, however: over-indulgence will turn the cat into a high-speed faecal factory and do it no good at all.

Diarrhoea should cause concern if it is either persistent or recurrent. The latter can be a symptom of a tumour in older cats and is present in a number of diseases. More often, however, diarrhoea is the result of a minor upset and is best treated by withholding food for a day and then feeding beaten raw egg, a little kaolin or other binding food. The motion itself may contain evidence of a more serious problem. Is the cat also passing blood? If so, consult the vet forthwith. Are there any signs of worms? Diarrhoea, especially in kittens, may be an indication of their presence. If you suspect anything more than a minor upset, scoop up a sample, place it in a sealed jar or container and ask the vet to have it examined microscopically.

Vomiting

Cats, like us, are sick from time to time. There is no reason to panic; overindulgence may easily be the cause. You should, however, check the vomit to see whether it really is the result of eating something indigestible. If the vomit is merely a sausage shape of food then the cat probably ate its last meal too fast – and may well have done if another cat was trying to make off with its favourite titbit. All cats bring up balls of fur that they have swallowed when washing their coats, and sometimes feathers if they have been eating a bird.

If vomiting is recurrent then something may well be wrong and you should consult the vet. The same is true if it is especially severe, perhaps accompanied by spasms. In this case, suspect poisoning and head for the surgery without delay.

Tumours

Cats, especially elderly ones, are susceptible to a variety of forms of cancer and unfortunately many of them are malignant. Over half the cancers of cats affect the alimentary system (though less frequently affecting the stomach than in humans) or the skin, and in females the reproductive system. Leukaemia has already been mentioned (see page 99). Some cancers are operable but in most cases little can be done, apart from surgery if that is possible. Chemotherapy has occasionally been tried, as has X-ray therapy – but the expense is usually prohibitive, and neither treatment is very easy to obtain.

Cats also have their share of warts and cysts. If they cause no discomfort to the cat they can usually be ignored, but those in awkward places are best treated. A wart near the eye could cause conjunctivitis, for example, or one in an exposed position become damaged and introduce infection. The same is true of internal cysts. Females that show eccentric behaviour are sometimes discovered to have cysts on their ovaries and in such cases an ovariohysterectomy is usually performed.

Rheumatic conditions

Cats do not suffer from actual rheumatism, but occasionally they can develop a form of rheumatoid arthritis. This usually affects the smaller joints equivalent to human fingers and toes, resulting in partial immobilization and loss of condition. The problem can be alleviated with drugs but cannot be cured. Arthritis can also develop from bites that penetrate the joint, so any nasty-looking bites should always be checked by the vet.

Skin conditions

Routine physical checks of skin and coat during grooming have already been described (see page 49). Less common than the signs mentioned are scabby patches, usually starting around the base of the tail and spreading along both sides of the spine. These are a common form of eczema, once thought to result from an all-fish diet but now thought probably to result from an allergic reaction to flea bites – so also look out for fleas. Biting, scratching and licking to ease irritation produce rawness. Follow your vet's instructions for treatment.

Hair loss, usually beginning on the inside of the rear legs, may be due to hormonal imbalance, although there is a hereditary form in which a downy coat of hair is retained. Sometimes the hair breaks off and ring-like patches can be seen on the skin. This is ringworm. Sometimes its only visible symptom is excessive scurf, but under ultraviolet light the fungus gives off fluorescence. Veterinary treatment is necessary, and bedding and other materials in contact with the cat should be treated carefully to destroy the fungus spores, which can infect humans.

External parasites

Fleas

It is almost inevitable that any cat allowed outdoors, and many indoor ones, will at some time pick up a flea. Fortunately, fleas are a problem that an owner can recognize and treat with ease. You will see the cat scratch, you will find the flea excreta when you groom, and you will probably see the fleas themselves moving in the fur, if not on the sofa. If there are only a couple and you catch them before they multiply, you may be able to seize them with your fingers and squash them.

With very young kittens, even with a greater infestation, this is all you should do – even though the fleas may keep returning, especially around the eyes. Young kittens may react badly to a pesticide. For this reason a pregnant female that regularly picks up fleas should be treated when you decide she is close enough to labour to be kept inside (though she could still pick them up from other cats that go in and out).

The easiest treatment is a dusting powder or pesticide spray, but it is essential to check it is suitable for cats. If you have any doubt, check with your vet – or get your pesticide from him in the first place. Pyrethum, made from the flower heads of a type of chrysanthemum, is quite safe, but some others may be harmful at high concentrations or if used repeatedly. Any containing DDT, phenols, tars and several other chemicals are harmful, even fatal, for cats. Pesticides sold for garden use can be very dangerous, and others must be used strictly as directed.

To give the treatment, stand the cat on a clean sheet of paper, as described in 'Grooming' (page 49). Powder or spray the cat from the rear forwards against the lie of the fur, and work the preparation into the fur. Take great care not to get it into the cat's mouth or eyes. Comb through the fur, destroying any fleas that fall out, then brush out the powder so that as little as possible is left in the fur for the cat to swallow when it washes.

With a very bad infestation, start the treatment by putting the cat in a plastic bag with its head sticking through the opening and puff the pesticide inside. At least one more treatment will be necessary after a week or ten days to kill off any fleas that have hatched since from eggs still stuck to the fur. You also have to treat all the cats (and dogs) in the house, their bedding and any areas where they regularly rest – for it is there, rather than on the cat, that the fleas may have laid many of their eggs. For a really bad infestation you may have to have your house fumigated to get rid of fleas, so it is much better to deal with them as soon as they appear.

Flea collars are available, impregnated with a chemical, but they can do more harm than good if used continually on some cats, and cannot generally be recommended.

Lice, ticks and mites

Many flea treatments deal with these other parasites, though you are much less likely to be troubled with them. Lice are rarely present on a healthy cat, but may move in on a sick one, especially on the head. Pear-shaped, yellow-white and the size of a pinhead, they are easily missed but their eggs stick to the cat's fur like a powdering of flour. Treatment is as for fleas, concentrating on the areas affected.

Country cats may pick up sheep and cattle ticks from grass and low bushes. In some warm countries, including parts of Australia, there is a type that causes paralysis – though fortunately the cat recovers when the ticks are removed. The most likely places to find them are on the neck and ears and between the toes. Though only pinhead-size they can swell to one-quarter inch (1 cm) long, brown or bluish-grey lumps when engorged with blood. They can be removed with tweezers or your fingernails, but first dab them with ether or alcohol, which makes them loosen their grip – otherwise you may leave the head embedded in the skin, which will cause a sore.

There are a number of mites that can settle on cats. Rabbit mites, occasionally found, can be treated like ticks. Harvest mites may appear as clumps of orange specks in late summer and autumn, especially where the skin is thin and hairless. They are usually noticed more by the raw or scabby patches produced by the cat licking the irritation, and can be treated with pyrethum and other suitable pesticides.

Another type of mite causes cat mange: small bare patches that spread from the ears or face to the feet and neck, which become bald and corrugated, or sometimes only produce a dandruff. This is contagious to humans, and although the mite cannot survive long on your body it can cause considerable irritation while it does. Treatment is by dressing and should be supervised by your vet. If you develop itchy weals and blisters, unobserved mites on a cat showing no apparent symptoms may be the cause.

Maggots

Sick or very elderly cats that have trouble keeping themselves perfectly clean may be troubled by maggots, which hatch from the eggs of flies laid in wounds or around the anus of cats with diarrhoea. The maggots can produce toxins that are very harmful to the cat when they burrow under the skin. Clip away hair around an infestation and clean thoroughly with warm water and suitable disinfectant. Even if you think they are all destroyed, make periodic checks to ensure that more have not hatched from eggs you missed.

Ear mites

Common in young cats and not infrequent among adult ones that range free are infestations of *Otodectes cynotis*, a mite which lives in the external ear and seems equally at home on cats or dogs. A cat with only a mild infestation may show few signs of discomfort, but any infestation should be treated promptly as a serious one will cause the animal great irritation. The cat may scratch its ears frenziedly and so damage them. Meanwhile the ear reacts by producing a dark brown wax, which will be much more noticeable than the tiny grey mites. The discharge may solidify into a hard mass and if the cat opens up a wound bacterial infection may follow, producing pus and serious damage to the inner ear. The persistent shaking of the head can also rupture blood vessels and lead to swelling. Kittens are particularly susceptible to ear mites.

Persistent scratching of the ears, particularly if accompanied by shaking or scratching of the head, suggests an immediate inspection for tell-tale specks of mites and the brownish waxy discharge. Treatment of a mild infestation is simple – insecticidal ear drops. The vet will give the first dose and show you how to continue the treatment. Follow his instructions carefully: you must kill not only the mites but also their eggs, which will otherwise hatch and start the process over again. A proper check when grooming should reveal a problem like this before it becomes serious.

Internal parasites

Roundworms and tapeworms are the main internal parasites of cats, but there are others. There is the protozoan *Toxoplasma*, for example, which often produces no symptoms, and the single-celled parasite *Isospora*; fortunately both are rare. Two tiny intestinal worms – threadworms and wireworms – can occasionally cause problems, as can flukes picked up from infected raw fish. Lungworms are fairly common among country cats, but only serious infestations seem to worry them. Finally, there are hookworms, which attach themselves to the intestinal wall and can cause anaemia and diarrhoea. They are much more of a problem in hot, humid countries than in temperate lands such as the British Isles.

Roundworms

These creepy-crawlies, which include *Toxocara cati*, can usually be recognized as thin threads in faeces and vomit. In extreme cases they can grow into thick, white worms up to 4 in (10 cm) long. They live in the cat's intestines on already digested food and their eggs are excreted in the faeces. The eggs can survive for years, hatching only if ingested and passed to the intestines.

The larvae of *Toxocara cati* migrate through the blood to the liver or lungs and can even be carried in the milk of a nursing mother and so passed on to her kittens. Although adult cats may be able to tolerate them in their system, the larvae seriously weakens kittens, producing coughing or even pneumonia as they work their way through the lungs in the direction of the intestine.

Symptoms of an infestation include failure to put on weight despite a hearty appetite, a pot belly and dry, harsh fur, usually accompanied by vomiting or diarrhoea. The adult worms are easily destroyed with the right worming tablets, but not so the larvae, and kittens are at risk because they cannot be treated until at least two weeks old. You would be well advised to have your vet check for any infestation during a pregnancy and to keep a regular watch for signs of the worms themselves at all times. Careful hygiene and the cooking of food will reduce the risk of infection.

Tapeworms

Tapeworms rarely have a noticeable effect on a cat's health, although they can cause a general loss of condition. In order to satisfy the demanding host lodged in its intestine, an infected cat will show a voracious appetite, often accompanied by digestive upsets. The segments of the worm break off and are expelled in the faeces, which is when you are most likely to be aware of them. They resemble long grains of rice, near the anus. If the cat seems to have an irritation around its rear end, keep an eye out for them.

Treatment is by worming tablets, but you should ask your vet to inspect the cat first. There are several different

kinds of tapeworm and effective medication has to be matched to the right type and the degree of infestation. One type of worm spends part of its life cycle in the cat flea, so have your pet treated for fleas at the same time, along with any other animals in the home.

Looking after a sick cat

Sick cats may welcome some comforting reassurance, but mainly they need rest and calm. Make sure you understand your vet's instructions and follow them precisely – it is amazing how many people stop a treatment before the period instructed because they think their animal is getting better, and thereby provoke relapse back into the condition.

A sick cat will probably want to retire to a quiet corner, but do not let it outside in case it hides away where you cannot find it to care for it. It will probably retire to its bed, but if it tries to hide, set up a sick bay somewhere sufficiently private.

Do not fuss a sick cat; make sure it is not in a draught and as comfortable as you can make it; change bedding if it becomes soiled, and take over all responsibility for grooming if the cat cannot keep itself clean.

A litter tray should be near by, and if a cat is too sick to reach it, carry it there several times a day. Support it if it is too weak to stand up alone, and clean its rear if it becomes soiled.

In most cases such assistance will be unnecessary – you will simply be required to give medication.

Giving pills

A person to assist you will make the pill-giving process less traumatic for you and your cat. Have your helper restrain the cat while you place one hand over the top of its head with the index finger and thumb coming forward on either side of the mouth. Squeeze gently at the corners of the mouth and the cat should 'open wide'. With the other hand, pop the pill as far back on the tongue as possible – some people like to use a wooden spatula to slip the pill past those sharp teeth! Now hold the mouth shut and stroke the throat in a downwards direction until you are quite certain the cat has swallowed. Do not let the cat go yet! Many become adept at pretending to swallow and spit the pill out later. Wait until the cat has opened its mouth and licked its lips, and keep an eye on it when you let it go – just in case!

If you have a gentle and amenable cat and have to give a pill on your own, you may be able to sit it on your lap, tummy up, and go through the same process. Difficult cats, however, may scrabble with their back claws to push your hands away. In this case, put a towel around the cat before you begin to restrain it.

Giving liquid medicines

It is not easy to give medicine by the spoonful, though you may be able to tug the cat's skin away from its lower teeth and tip a little in. Much better is to use a syringe (the kind that is used with a hypodermic needle – but without the needle, of course). Your vet will have a supply of disposable plastic syringes and will supply one. Fill it carefully (quantity can be gauged by the scale on the side), and insert it at the side of the cat's mouth where there is a gap in the teeth. Hold the mouth closed over it and squirt a little at a time so the cat does not choke (especially important with small kittens) and then follow the throat-stroking procedure. It is better to give medicines with the cat in a standing position.

The ageing cat

Sensible care, a balanced diet without overfeeding, and a friend ready to play games will keep your cat a lively kitten-cat for many years. Eventually, however, the signs of senior citizenship begin to appear. Veterinary treatments and a better understanding of feline needs have increased a cat's life expectancy from a typical twelve-year span to fifteen years or even longer – a very few to well past thirty. As with humans, extended life is really an extension of old age, and to make it a happy one you must take greater care of puss's needs.

When a cat begins to show its years is as variable as with humans, but with age cats need more rest, become even less tolerant of noise and disturbance, and cannot be expected to stay continent for long periods. They will not be able to cope with cold winter nights on the tiles, and even if they have been used to choosing their own loo they should be coaxed back to the litter box of their kittenhood – after all you would not expect grandma to use a toilet at the bottom of the garden on a wet winter night – and not shut out of the house.

Try to avoid putting elderly cats out to board, especially if they are not used to it. The experience will be unsettling and in turn that may cause physical deterioration. Elder cats are more susceptible to disease and not even the best-run cattery can stop the occasional bug arriving with a visitor.

Frequent grooming will become really necessary – a cat that feels clean and fresh will have more chance of feeling healthy – and you will probably have to pay more attention to keeping it clean. Claws are more likely to need trimming, and dead hair should be removed so that fur ball formation is avoided when the cat is washing.

Veterinary check-ups should be at least every six months so that any disorder can be spotted before it becomes a

problem. Tartar will need to be scaled from teeth more often, and if a cat has to have its teeth removed you will have to chop up food. If there are digestive problems you may have to follow a special diet. For kidney trouble – and nephritis is a terminal illness for many cats – you will have to wean your cat off red meat. Vitamins and other supplements may be recommended. Sardines in oil once or twice a week will help to prevent constipation.

Euthanasia

When a cat has finally used up all of its nine lives (and it is no use trying to count them, for you do not know the risks it has encountered on its own!), there comes a time when it either gives up the struggle or becomes so severely ill that to continue its pain would be cruel. If there is no hope of cure and the cat is in distress, or if the cure is so uncertain and involves great pain or, perhaps, in certain circumstances, where the treatment would be so costly or the aftercare so demanding that an owner cannot cope – the cat's life can be ended painlessly. Today this is usually carried out by a simple injection into a vein of an instantly lethal drug. Beyond the initial prick the cat feels nothing, and is dead within a couple of seconds. Terminating a cat's life is never an easy decision to take, but the owner is the one to feel distress – the cat may react to the tension of its owner, but, since the experience has not happened before and is not performed in front of other cats, there are no grounds for supposing that the cat knows what is going to happen. If it is in great pain it would probably not survive for long on its own anyway, and if you have seen increasing sickness and weakness develop it is likely that you, as a caring owner, will help your cat to a peaceful end with a sense of relief.

Disposal of the remains can be left to your vet, who will arrange for incineration or collection. Local regulations may permit burial in your own garden (in which case the grave should be at least 3 ft (90 cm) deep), and in some places pet funeral parlours and burial grounds offer their services with tributes and memorials according to the owner's taste and pocket. Whether you endow a veterinary hospital in your cat's memory, or simply put a coin in the can on animal charity days, the best memorial of all will be the memories of many happy hours together.

8. First aid

Cats are cautious and do not usually take unnecessary risks. They are also very curious and the world is full of dangers, from the juggernaut on the main road to the threaded needle on the carpet, the dog next door to the pot plant on the table. Every owner should know how to deal with minor injuries and administer first aid, though the untrained should not usually attempt more than that. If you do not know what to do to help an injured cat then it is better to do nothing other than see that it does not injure itself further and get professional help straight away. However, immediate first aid treatment can often make a minor contribution to its recovery.

Handling an injured cat

A cat that has been hurt in an accident or by some misadventure will be in pain and frightened. It will be defensive and not likely to be a co-operative patient, especially if you are a stranger. Even a cat that comes to you, its trusted owner, asking for help with a thorn in the paw, or some similar injury, may forget that you are trying to help and lash out with a claw because you hurt in helping. Naturally, you will talk soothingly to the cat and try to gain its confidence, but a towel or coat wrapped around it will restrain it and a pair of gloves will give protection from teeth and claws. A caring owner, dashing into action, may think a few savage bites and scratches small pains if he or she can help the cat, but such wounds should not be ignored. Cats' mouths often contain bacteria which can invade a bite wound and, especially if you have not had an antitetanus injection within three years, wounds should be soaked in hot water containing antiseptic and seen by a nurse or doctor. If infection does develop antibiotics may be needed.

Accidents

These come in all shapes and sizes, but those involving motor vehicles are usually the worst. An untrained person will not be able to tell what injuries have been sustained by a cat struck by a car and should not attempt to treat them except to stem any bleeding. Then get the animal to the vet as soon as possible – and *not*, if it can be avoided, the other way round. It is almost always quicker for you to take the animal *to* the vet, and if you have warned him that you are on your way he will have time to prepare for emergency action.

The first thing to do immediately after any accident is to keep the victim calm and confined; even a badly injured animal may try to drag itself away to imagined safety. There will almost certainly be shock, producing rapid, shallow breathing and a feeble pulse, often with dilated pupils. Quiet and warmth are the best treatment.

To move an injured cat, lift it by the scruff of the neck to avoid clawing if it is conscious, supporting its rump with your other hand. If the cat is lying on its side and offers no resistance, tuck your hands under its shoulders and pelvis. Either way, the important thing is to keep the cat as still as possible, to avoid exacerbating any internal injuries or causing new ones. Then lay the cat on a blanket or coat, folding it in if it struggles, and place the bundle in a basket or box if one is to hand. You should try to keep the animal's head lower than the rest of the body to ensure circulation of blood to the brain.

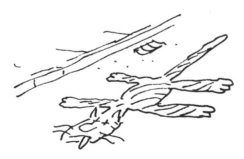

Heavy bleeding can be staunched with a pad of cotton wool or a folded handkerchief. If this is ineffective apply a tourniquet (see page 115), but do so on the way to the vet – don't delay your journey by struggling with cloth or belt.

Cats are also at risk of falling from considerable heights. Such falls can often cause severe internal damage as well as obvious external injury and should be treated in the same way as other serious accidents.

Sometimes the cat may seem all right after a fall, get up and walk away, but look out for any sign of broken limbs. In bad falls a cat sometimes dislocates its jaw, which will be evident because it will not be able to close its mouth properly, or may fracture its hard palate. The injury to the roof of the mouth will probably not be evident until mealtime when the cat only takes a little food, then flicks its tongue up to lick food out of its nostrils. With the mouth open you may see a split in the palate which the vet will have to stitch together.

Fights

A cat's fur gives some protection from injury in a fight, but it also hides injuries that have been sustained and which may go unnoticed when the cat comes home. If your cat comes rushing home with its tail fluffed out and looking frightened watch out for any concentrated washing of a particular part of its body a few hours later, a possible sign that it has sustained a wound there, and check the area for damage.

Cats' wounds usually heal rapidly, but if one goes unnoticed it may heal over dirt or infection, leaving an abscess to develop. Bigger wounds and injuries will be more noticeable from the start. Dog bites can be deep and dangerous and will usually tear the flesh, but cat and rodent bites are often puncture wounds. They may pass notice until an abscess forms a few days later, evident as a swelling. The cat will probably be in pain and generally off colour. If the abscess develops it may burst, releasing pus or even a patch of fur and dead skin.

To treat an abscess yourself you must draw out the pus with a pad of lint or cotton wool soaked in hot salt-water, made up of a teaspoon of salt to a pint (half a litre) of boiling water (if the water is not too hot for you it will not be too hot for the cat). Hold the pad against the infected area until it begins to lose its heat, then soak it again and repeat the process. On a limb it may be easier to immerse the whole leg, if the cat co-operates. When the abscess has burst, switch to using dilute hydrogen peroxide instead of a saline solution and continue bathing. The peroxide both helps get the pus out and counteracts its smell so that the cat is less likely to bother the wound. Finish bathing with salt-water.

It is difficult to remove all the pus from an abscess in one go, which means that periodic bathing will be required for several days. It is far better, in fact, to get the cat to the vet if you think an abscess is coming to a head. He will be able to lance or burst it properly and apply anti-biotics if necessary, for some abscesses can be serious. An abscess between the shoulders, for example, over a joint or on the tail, near the eyes or on the jaw or ear will need antibiotics and skilled veter-inary treatment from the start to avoid permanent damage.

Dealing with wounds

In a case of serious accident, when pro-fessional attention is urgently required, do not stop to clean up a wound, unless a piece of glass or other object is easily removed, but concentrate instead on stemming bleeding. Scratches and minor lacerations should be cleaned with a salt solution or dilute hydrogen peroxide, *never* with strong antiseptics made for humans; they could irritate the tissues and actually delay healing and may interfere with any antibiotics. If you can get a wound treated by the vet within a day it is probably better not to cover it.

Bleeding

Pressure directly on a wound, either with the hand or using a pad of cloth, will help stem bleeding. On a limb the wound could be covered with a layer of lint or gauze, then a pad of cotton wool, and tightly bandaged from the foot upwards.

In serious cases a tourniquet can be applied *between* the wound and the body to reduce arterial blood reaching it from the heart. A handkerchief will serve. Knot it around the limb or tail, push a pencil or similar object through the knot and twist it to tighten the grip. A tour-niquet must be loosened at intervals of not more than fifteen minutes, for to cut off the blood supply for longer could lead to gangrene and other problems.

Sometimes a blow may cause bleeding beneath the skin without breaking its surface, producing a blood blister or haematoma. In minor cases it may be sufficient to apply a cold compress to reduce the swelling, but in bad ones the vet may need to drain the blister or even cut the skin away for healing. If the cat is scratching the swelling (and haematomas on the ear are often the result of persistent scratching because of an ear infection) cover the area with a dry dressing or, in the case of ears, fit an Elizabethan collar (see below).

Bandages

Most cats do not much like bandages and try to pull them off, so they must be securely fixed. Your vet probably will not expect you to replace dressings, for doing so himself will provide an opportunity to check the condition of the wound. In any case, if the cat manages to get a professionally applied bandage off it is unlikely that an amateur attempt will stay on better. However, to deal with emergencies and to keep the cat from worrying wounds if it does manage to get a bandage off, here is what you should do.

The equipment in the human medicine chest will serve, with the tubular bandages designed for fingers and thumbs being especially useful on feline feet. Do not, however, use already treated dressings which may include antiseptics harmful to cats.

Always bandage as smoothly and flatly as possible, without using knots, and bandage over a wider area than the wound itself: even if it is quite a small area of the head or body it will be necessary to wrap the whole to keep the bandages secure. On the head, for example, start below the chin, carry the bandage over the head in front of one ear and behind the other, back under the chin and then round again as necessary. If you have a wider bandage take it over the top of the head, cutting a hole for the ears to poke through.

Secure the finished bandage with sticking plaster, and if you want it to stay on for some time tape all the edges to the fur. This is always more secure than tying knots in the conventional way. To bandage an ear itself you need to bandage front and back of it, then pad the ear on either side with plenty of cotton wool and secure it to the bandages by covering all with sticky tape.

You can bandage the body by wrapping it vertically and then carrying one end of the roll back to the tail and around its base, where it can be secured. Alternatively use a piece of cloth, cut holes for the limbs if it is to extend that far and snip the side edges into vertical strips. Then you can pop the feet through the holes, draw the cloth up the sides of the cat and tie the strips to each other along the spine.

To bandage a paw, start by padding between the toes with small pieces of cotton wadding and a larger one under the pad, then bring a bandage down from above the wound, over the end of the paw and back up the leg. Wrap the bandage in a spiral downwards and back up again spiralling the opposite way. A tubular bandage is much easier: slide it over the limb, fold the bottom end back over the paw and secure with sticky tape, then secure the top end to the fur. A tail can be bandaged like a paw but along its whole length, securing it at the base with sticking plaster and then covering the whole with tape.

Bootees made from tubular bandage and taped over the paws are useful to stop a cat from scratching at a wound or trying to tear a bandage off. To protect the head from scratching, or to stop the cat from biting at bandages, you will have to go one stage further and make the cat an Elizabethan collar. Cut a circle about 12 in (30 cm) in diameter from some thick but flexible card. Cut out a big hole in the centre about 4 in (10 cm) across and then chop out an arc slightly more than a quarter of the circle. Make some holes at equal distances down each side of the two edges where you cut the arc away and put pieces of sticking plaster around the edge of the inner circle to soften it. Now wrap the contraption around the cat's neck and thread a lace or piece of string through the holes to pull it into a funnel shape. Adjust for fit if necessary, stand back and hope for the best.

If you are lucky you may not have to go to all this trouble, for these collars are now being made in plastic or fibreglass to fit on the cat's own collar. They are more cat-proof than card, so it is worth putting up with their one disadvantage – if the cat scratches away at them all night they make a dreadful noise!

Fractures

A fracture can range from a cracked toe to a shattered spine. Traffic accidents, awkward falls from a height (especially if the cat is half asleep or concentrating on something else), a bad encounter with a dog or deliberate human cruelty are likely causes – but a small kitten could break a bone (often one of the lower bones of the front legs) just jumping out of your arms.

Amateur treatment of fractures can do more harm than good. If a cat has multiple injuries, likely if it has been hit by a car or savaged by a dog, it is much more important to staunch bleeding and get it to the vet. The time taken to get professional attention will not affect recovery from a simple fracture. Only if you have absolutely no access to a vet should you attempt to treat a fracture by, say, splinting a limb with a flat piece of wood on either side and securing the whole with bandages.

It is as well, however, to be able to recognize a possible fracture. If a kitten limps after jumping or falling out of your arms, for example, check the injured leg. If it seems floppy and is obviously painful head straight to the vet. A simple bruise is more likely if the limb seems all right and the kitten is walking on it a few hours later.

To test for a suspected broken limb, get someone else to place the cat down gently on a table while you compare the suspected limb with its partner. Do they hang differently, or look different lengths? Ask your assistant to hold the cat by the scruff of the neck and to put a hand beneath its chest to take its weight. By lifting the hand a little the weight is transferred to the rear. Does the cat take all the weight on one leg and flinch as the other touches the table? To check the front legs, move the cat towards the edge of the table. Most cats will instinctively reach out for the edge. If it pulls itself forwards with the suspect leg you can be fairly sure that it is not broken.

Burns and scalds

The instant treatment for a general burn is to douse the affected area with cold water, then apply a pad soaked in cold water and get the cat to the vet as rapidly as possible. Even more important is to treat the animal for shock by keeping it still and quiet. Burns to the paw pads, usually from jumping on to a cooker hotplate or other heated surface, should be smothered with Vaseline and wrapped with soft cloth. Do not attempt to bandage them.

Cats generally learn from experience to avoid hot surfaces – once burned twice shy – but scalds are much more frequent and usually not the cat's fault. Take particular care that pan handles do not project where they can be knocked and that kettles are not overfilled so that they boil over. A cat's fur does give some protection and a minor scald can be soothed by smothering with olive oil or Vaseline. The problem is that since the fur is not singed the injury from a liquid scald may not be apparent; even fat may be licked off by the cat. If the skin dies and falls off, leaving a raw patch, this will need very careful attention.

Chemical burns, from corrosive and caustic substances, may take some days before injury becomes visible, though the mouth and tongue can be damaged in trying to lick them off. If you see a cat splashed by or walk into acid (a leak from a car battery, perhaps) mix some bicarbonate of soda in a bucket of water, put on some gloves and push the cat into the bucket as quickly as possible to dilute the acid. For caustic substances use boric acid instead of bicarbonate. If you do not know what has caused a burn use water, wrap the cat in a blanket and get it to the vet for immediate treatment.

Foreign objects

Bones or other objects may get caught on the teeth or in the throat. If you can see them remove with tweezers. Needles can be particularly dangerous if swallowed, so do not leave threaded ones about. And if you see a piece of cotton hanging from a cat's anus do *not* pull it – there may be a needle or part of one on the other end, and even if there is not you could damage the rectal lining in pulling out the thread. Cut it short about 1½ in (4 cm) from the anus so the cat cannot play with it and arrange for a trip to the vet.

If a cat is limping, check the paw for a piece of broken glass, a thorn or some other object that may have penetrated it. Even a grass seed can work its way under the skin between the toes and cause a suppurating sore. Extract the offending article with tweezers if you can, bathe the wound and keep an eye open for any signs of infection.

Foreign objects in an eye or ear will almost certainly need veterinary attention if they have worked their way under the skin or below the nictating membrane. You should never try to remove an object embedded in the eye, although you will probably be able to wipe away a speck of dust, say, with the corner of a handkerchief. The same is true of ears: do *not* go poking around down the ear canal; confine any treatment to wiping external parts only with a damp cloth.

Stings

Some cats seem immune to wasp and bee stings, but stings on the lips or chin when trying to catch an insect may swell up and hamper breathing. Try to find the sting and remove it with tweezers or by pressing it out with your fingernails (mind the cat does not bite you). Antihistamine ointment may help. If a sting is near the eye leave it to the vet.

Poisons

Cats seldom eat poisons accidentally, but they can easily get poisonous substances on their coats and ingest them accidentally when washing. Keep household poisons out of their way (see page 23 for some typical examples). If you know that rodent poisons are used frequently in your neighbourhood, find out the antidote and keep some to hand, just in case.

An improvised general antidote that can be used in an emergency is strong tea, milk of magnesia and burned toast (or charcoal), all mixed together. A kitten should be made to swallow at least one to two teaspoonfuls and an adult twice as much. Failing that, hydrogen peroxide (one part peroxide to 12 parts water) or a salt solution will do as emetics. Do not try to induce vomiting if the mouth appears burned.

It hardly needs to be said that garden weedkillers or insecticides should not be used where there are cats about.

Snake and spider bites

If you live in an area where there are poisonous snakes, spiders or scorpions, you probably know the drill for humans: tourniquet the wound to try to stop poison from entering the system, pack ice around the swelling, and get treatment with the appropriate antiserum as soon as possible. Poisons spread rapidly through the smaller body of the cat, so no time can be wasted.

Heat exhaustion

Although cats are fairly resilient to changes in temperature, heat exhaustion can be a serious affair unless treated promptly. It is really only likely to occur in hot weather, especially if the animal is confined in airless quarters. The reason for this will probably be inadvertent – a nosy individual mistakenly shut in a cupboard, for example.

A cat suffering from heat exhaustion will be in obvious distress – panting, perhaps vomiting and certainly in shock. Act quickly to cool the animal down. Douse it with cold water or, better, plunge it into a bathful packed with ice. As soon as the cat has recovered sufficiently, get it to the vet.

Drowning

Open the cat's mouth and pull its tongue forward, then, standing with your legs apart, hold its back legs and let it hang in front of you and swing it forwards to the horizontal and back between your legs. This will drain any water and, hopefully, start it breathing. If this does not start respiration, try the 'kiss of life': place your mouth over the cat's mouth and nose, and blow and release; or, with the cat's tongue still held extended, make a cup around the jaws to blow through.

Electric shock

First, switch off the power – and be careful that you do not make contact with a puddle of pee in reaching the switch, for the cat will probably urinate and urine carries electricity. If you cannot switch off the electricity, pull the cat away with a stick or some other nonconductive object. If the cat is not breathing apply artificial respiration as for drowning (above). Electric shock can also cause heart failure and, since it is usually due to cats chewing through a wire, burns around the mouth, so veterinary attention may be required urgently.

9. Showing off

Some general comments about the various types of cat have already been made in the first chapter, but it should be emphasized again that cats are much more alike than they are different, and most of the information in this book applies to them all. Given that long fur requires more grooming and lack of fur demands protection from the cold – there is one very rare breed of cat, the Sphinx, that has only a slight down except for a few longer strands over its testicles – appearance is more a matter of taste than a guide to what a particular kind of cat will be like to live with. After all, you do not judge a person's intelligence or friendliness by the length of their hair, the shape of their ears, the shade of their eyes or the colour of their skin – and it would be just as foolish to attempt to do so with a cat. Individual family background and upbringing make a much bigger difference.

However, an American, an Italian, a Japanese and a Moroccan will all have totally different cultural backgrounds, and these, much more than their physical differences, will influence the development of their personalities. It can be much the same with cats.

It is not reliable to take a breed name as an indication of an animal's origin. Historians of the cat world will long dispute whether the Abyssinian had anything to do with Ethiopia, or the Russian really come from Russia, but the three broad types of Longhair (Persian), Shorthair and Foreign Shorthair (Oriental) do generally fit the broad characteristics already described. People attracted to a particular breed may also share a common attitude to cats and similar expectations of them, so the way they treat them reinforces particular characteristics, conditioning playing as much a part as heredity.

To be recognized as an official breed a type has to be produced that 'breeds true', which means that kittens must exactly

resemble their parents. A certain number of cats must be bred – and agreement reached that the cat is really sufficiently different – before it can be declared official and given breed status. In Britain, the whole cat world is organized under one body, the Governing Council of the Cat Fancy (or was until a breakaway faction developed to encourage a wider range of breeds), but in North America there are a number of competing organizations that make their own rules; the situation varies from country to country. For that reason some types are recognized in one country but not in another; one organization may place a cat in a breed of its own whereas another may consider it only a colour variation. Since there are over 300 different breeds recognized in Britain and America alone, this is not the place to give a detailed description of them. However, it is worth knowing a little of how the Cat Fancy describes breeds of different kinds and, indeed, about the breeds themselves so that you can decide which one will be the most suitable for you.

Short-haired cats

Short fur is the normal length for cats. No wild cats have long hair, not even those living in cold climates – although their short hair is very thick. Short hair is always genetically dominant in cats, which means that if your charming, long-haired Burmese goes feral its descendants will revert to a short-haired state. Fur type and texture, and the exact length of the hair, vary between breeds with the result that 'short-haired' cats can look very different from one another. The sleeker, slimmer Oriental breeds are grouped separately as the Foreign Shorthairs; they are covered on pages 125–8.

British Shorthairs

The British Shorthair – and the European Shorthair, which is really just another name for the same type – is a sturdy, stocky animal officially described as compact, well balanced and powerful. It has a good depth of body, a full, broad chest and short, strong legs. The shortish tail is thick at the base and tapers a little to a rounded tip. The paws are rounded and the head, too, is rounded and also massive, shaped almost like an apple with full cheeks, a short broad nose and small ears with rounded tips, set well apart. The eyes are big and round. The ideal British Shorthair has a coat like plush velvet and can be a variety of colours and patterns.

The colour known as the British Blue (see page 93) is the variety that most frequently approaches the requirements laid down as ideal; the breed has a reputation for being very placid and gentle. The colour should be even all over and extend to the roots of the fur; in show cats, a light to medium blue is preferred. All-over colours (self-coloured cats as they are known technically) can also be white, black, cream or red; a range of tabby colours in two kinds of pattern; spotted; a mixture of black, red and pale red, or of blue and cream; white patched with one of the solid colours, or a patchwork of black, red and white; or, finally, with an undercoat of white fur and a topcoat tipped with one of the colours or patterns listed already. Enough variation for you?

Almost all these cats have eyes of copper, orange or deep gold, except for the white-haired ones which may have blue eyes, or one eye blue and the other orange, and the Silver Tabbies and Silver Spotted kinds which have green or hazel eyes. In a proper pedigree cat, the skin of the nose – or 'nose leather' to use the unlovely official term – and the skin of the paw pads should match the colour of the coat.

The immense variety of British Shorthairs reflects their excellence as pets. They are intelligent, affectionate and loyal; most are very playful and good with children, even with dogs if they have to share their home with one. They conduct themselves with dignity and aplomb, are fairly undemanding in their needs and so make ideal companions for the novice cat owner.

Manx

The Manx is essentially a British Shorthair with no tail – or, at least, it used to be. Short-tailed and fully tailed versions are now bred, and in the United States five different breed types have been accepted: Rumpy (no tail), Riser (with a small number of tail vertebrae that can be felt or seen), Stubby (with a short but movable tail), Longy (with a longer but still less than full tail) and Tailed (with a normal tail). The Manx also has a distinctive kind of fur, with a thick undercoat and a longer topcoat. Its hind legs are longer than the front ones, giving it a rather hopping gait like that of a rabbit.

While one may question the elegance of the names for the various types, it is perhaps fortunate that this peculiar cat has had its missing appendage at least partially restored. Because taillessness is linked with spinal problems in the breed, there is a high mortality rate in Manx kittens; and if two tailless Manx are bred the kittens are rarely born alive. To avoid this, Manx cats are now always bred to tailed ones – hence the range of tail lengths now recognized officially, all of which could appear in a litter. Coat colours can be any of those for other Shorthairs, except for the Siamese pattern.

Manx cats are generally agreed to have originated on the Isle of Man in the Irish Sea, although how they got there in the first place is a matter of considerable speculation. They are an intelligent and easily trained breed.

American Shorthairs

American Shorthairs were known formerly as Domestic Shorthairs and sometimes still are. They are similar to their

British counterparts and developed from the same stock, but today North American standards require a somewhat longer-looking cat than the British kind and with a less rounded head – more of a heart shape and with slightly larger ears. The American Shorthair has fur of a much harsher texture and displays some colour variations not known in Britain, among them Calico, a white cat patched with black and red, and the Dilute Calico, which is blue and cream on white. American Shorthairs are renowned for their hunting ability and are said to be good mousers.

American Wirehair

This resembles an American Shorthair but with fur like that of a wire-haired terrier dog, especially on the head, back, sides and top of the tail. The fur is softer on the chin and belly. The breed is the result of a chance mutation, in 1966, that produced a wire-haired kitten in a litter born in New York State. Despite its short history, the American Wirehair has gained rapid popularity, perhaps because it is one of the very few breeds that can be said to be American born and bred.

Exotic Shorthair

This is another American cat with short fur but of a more silky texture than that of the American Shorthair. Its physique is closer to that of the long-haired or Persian cat, which is hardly surprising as the breed was established in the 1960s by crossing a Persian with an American Shorthair. This has also led to its distinctly rounded head and short nose. Exotic Shorthairs are ideal city cats, gentle, expressive and quite content to lie by the fire or sprawl on a soft cushion.

Rex cats

The fur of this distinctive breed differs from that of all other cats. It contains a unique balance of straight and curly hairs that results in a curly coat; those unaware of this may otherwise suppose that the cat has been subjected to very peculiar treatment in a beauty parlour. Isolated instances of this coat mutation have appeared in North America and Germany, but most true Rex are descended from cats which appeared in the two adjoining counties of Devon and Cornwall in south-west England. In fact the Devon and Cornish races are genetically distinct and if interbred produce offspring with straight coats. As this could be a matter of some disappointment to an expectant breeder unable to distinguish between the two, the Devon Rex has been further bred to have a differently shaped head, with prominent cheeks and large, oval-shaped ears. This makes it look rather like a four-legged pixie, but at least there is no longer an excuse for confusing it with its Cornish cousin.

Rex cats can be any of the standard colours or patterns, including Siamese Colourpoint, in which case they are known as the Si-Rex.

Scottish Fold

This is another breed with a physical

peculiarity. The Scottish Fold has flopped-down ears, which produce its rather surprised and melancholy expression. The breed originated from a kitten born with floppy ears on a farm in Scotland in 1961, but it has never been recognized in Britain; the main following is in North America. Scottish Fold kittens are born with ordinary, pricked-up ears; the distinctive folded appearance develops as the kittens grow.

Foreign Shorthairs

These cats, often known as Orientals, are neither oriental nor particularly foreign – perhaps like chop suey, which originated in North America. Although some Orientals may have had an Eastern origin, most owe their development to Western breeders. Almost all have rather slim, elegant bodies with slim legs and long, tapering tails. Their heads tend to a wedge shape with large, pointed ears and almond-shaped eyes. Most of them are cats that demand attention; they need owners prepared to treat them as partners and to share lots of activities. Should such attention not be forthcoming, most Orientals will make known their displeasure in no uncertain manner.

Siamese

This is the best known of the Oriental cats. With its elegant form and distinctive pattern of pale fur with darker colouring on the limbs, tail, face and ears, the Siamese (see page 41) has long been kept and admired all over the world. It has a long body, a slim, tapering tail, long legs with dainty oval paws and a wedge-shaped head with slanted almond-shaped eyes and large pointed ears. Siamese are lively, demanding and talkative, and will expect the same qualities from you. This is very much a 'people-orientated' breed and most Siamese are particularly loyal to their owner and household; strangers may be treated with complete indifference. Siamese have a high-pitched and intrusive miaow, especially when in heat.

The points, as the patches of colour are known, may be seal (actually a dilution of black), chocolate, blue, red, cream, lilac, tabby or tortoiseshell.

Foreign Selfs/Oriental Shorthairs

Cats identical to the Siamese but with solidly coloured coats instead of the point markings are known in Britain as the Foreign White, Foreign Black and Foreign Lilac. There is provisional official recognition for coat colours in red, cream and cinnamon; tabby, tortoiseshell and tipped coats also have preliminary standards. Note that Oriental Shorthairs is the name used in North America.

Colourpoint Shorthairs

This is the name given in North America to the tabby (or lynx point) and tortoiseshell varieties of the Siamese. Some organizations do not accept them as examples of the pure breed.

Burmese

The Burmese is a heavier cat than the Siamese – and is heavier than it looks – with a rounded chest and a medium-length tail that tapers only slightly and has a rounded tip. The head, too, is more rounded and tapers to a short, blunt wedge with full, wide cheeks. The ears tilt forwards and, in North American specimens, the eyes and paws are distinctly round. In Britain the eyes have an oriental slant and the feet are oval. The Burmese has a brown to sable-brown coat, although a wide range of other colours are recognized in Britain, rather fewer in the United States. This is a most attractive breed: healthy, affectionate and intelligent, adaptable and good with people. It likes to play, and its owner should, too.

Tonkinese

The Tonk, as it is sometimes called, is a North American hybrid between a Siamese and a Burmese, thus showing characteristics that are a blend of those of its parents. The most common colour is natural mink – warm brown with darker points – but three other colours are also bred: honey mink, champagne and blue.

Havana Brown

In Britain the Havana (or Havana Brown as it is known in the United States) is a cat of Siamese type with a rich chestnut-brown coat; it was known for a time as the Chestnut Foreign Shorthair. In the United States the breed has a more rounded muzzle and round-tipped ears, and does not look nearly so like its relative, the Siamese. A well-bred Havana Brown should have an elegant, muscular body and oval-shaped green eyes. This is one of the most attractive breeds: playful, aristocratic, loyal and home-loving. Like the Siamese, it is very much a one-person cat.

Abyssinian

An exotic cat with an exotic name, the forerunners of the breed were reputedly brought to England from Abyssinia in the middle of the nineteenth century. Since then its popularity has gone from strength to strength. The Abyssinian (see page 43) is heavier than the Siamese and is noticeable for its 'agouti' coat in which each hair is tipped or striped along its length with darker colour. The breed is now recognized in a number of colours, including Ruddy (golden brown with black tipping), Sorrel (copper red with chocolate tipping), Blue (tipped with darker blue) and is provisionally accepted in Chocolate, Lilac, Fawn, Silver, Sorrel/Silver (silvery peach) and Blue/Silver varieties. The underparts shade to a lighter colour and there are dark, pale-edged vertical lines on the forehead.

The Abyssinian is a playful cat, although some individuals can act more like hell-raisers; it certainly takes a great interest in everything that goes on. Note, however, that the breed is in heavy demand, will not come cheap and needs plenty of space outdoors, where it loves to climb trees.

Russian Blue

This is not so extreme in type as the Siamese (and is even less so in the United States). The breed's distinctive character is its soft, silky coat with a silvery sheen; the hairs are thick and perfectly uniform, giving excellent protection in cold conditions. The blue-grey coat gives the breed its name, but other solid colours have now been recognized. This is a genial, happy cat without a hint of eponymous melancholy and is well suited to a city house or apartment.

Korat

This breed comes from the Korat region of Thailand. Its silver-blue coat is soft, thick, glossy and silver-tipped. The cat has a more heart-shaped head than the Siamese and particularly large and luminous eyes. As befits its ancient and aristocratic origins, the breed likes calm and well-organized surroundings. This is not a cat to consider if your house is full of children and dogs, though in Thailand the toms are said to be tough fighters.

Egyptian Mau

The origins of the Egyptian Mau are said to go back to the time of the pharaohs; certainly, it resembles the cats shown in Egyptian wall paintings. The modern origins of the breed, however, date back only to the 1950s, when an individual was imported from Egypt to the United States. The cat has a distinctive spotted coat, is heavier than the Siamese and its head is a more rounded wedge. The

markings on the face are more like lines and the tail is banded. This is an American-raised breed, not to be confused with a similar, British cat also once known as the Mau, which is of a more Siamese type and is now known officially as the Oriental Spotted Tabby, as it was created during the development of the Tabby Point Siamese. The Egyptian Mau is an adaptable but delicate breed: make sure you have the time to look after it if you decide to buy one.

Japanese Bobtail

This is another curio, a cat from the orient but not of the usual Oriental type. Its chief characteristic is the tail from which it takes its name. This is short, usually about 4 in (10 cm) long, and curls back on itself – so appearing even shorter. It is also covered with hairs that seem to grow in every direction. This is an unusual arrangement; the uncharitable might say that it resembles a cross between the bobble of a tam-o'-shanter and a rabbit's scut – but the Japanese Bobtail is quite normal in all other respects and makes a congenial companion. Apart from the tail the fur is soft, silky and of medium length. Black, white or red are the preferred colours, either all over or in patches.

Long-haired cats

No wild members of the cat family have long hair resembling that of the domesticated cat. It is the result of centuries of careful (perhaps more often not so careful) breeding. Actually, 'long-haired' is a blanket term for a variety of breeds whose coats can differ considerably in length and texture. Here are some of the more interesting ones.

Angora

This was probably the first kind of long-haired cat to be seen in Europe. The Angora arrived in the sixteenth century, probably from Turkey (it takes its name from the Turkish capital, Ankara). It gradually lost favour to the Persian (see below) and the breed was dwindling fast until a few specimens were taken to the United States from Ankara Zoo. It has a longish body and tail, long legs with

neat, dainty paws and a small head with large almond-shaped eyes that slope slightly upwards and large upright ears. Its fur is gorgeously textured, like mohair. White was the only acceptable colour when the breed was re-established in the United States, but other colours are now being bred in both Europe and North America.

Longhair or Persian

This breed has a short and massive body set on short thick legs with a short tapering tail. The head is round and broad with a short nose and full cheeks, large round eyes and small ears set low and far apart. The long luxuriant fur forms a ruff around the neck and over the top of the chest and the tail is, as they say, full. It comes in many colours, in solid, tabby, tipped, such as the Chinchilla (see page

42), and patched patterns. This is an exceptionally attractive and affectionate cat that looks, and likes to be, pampered – which includes regular care of its luxuriant coat. Watch out for confusion over names when buying: in Britain the breed is known officially as the Longhair, but as the Persian in North America.

Colourpoint Longhair or Himalayan

These are long-haired (Persian) cats with a coat pattern like that of the Siamese; and like the Siamese, a range of different colours are now accepted. The breed is entirely man-made, being created this century by crossing the Siamese and the Persian. Beware of the name if you decide to buy: the breed is known as the Colourpoint Longhair in Britain but as the Himalayan in North America, and it should not be confused with the Colourpoint Shorthair, which is the North American name for one of the Oriental-type cats.

Birman

This delightful breed (see page 42) is superficially rather like the Colourpoint Longhair. However, it has a rather longer look overall and the most distinctive difference is that the dark colouring of the Birman's legs does not extend over the paws, which are white, as though the cat had stepped into a bowl of milk.

Turkish Cat

A sturdy individual that really does come from Turkey, this one has a wedge-shaped head, although not so long as that of the Siamese, with round amber eyes and large upright ears. The full coat is chalk white with auburn patches on the ears extending to the face but leaving a white blaze between. Its auburn tail is ringed with darker shading. Names here are even more confusing than usual. Turkish Cat is now the officially recognized name, but the breed was once known as the Turkish Van because it came from near Lake Van in that country. It should be distinguished from the Angora and especially from the Turkish Angora, a name not officially recognized in Britain but which may occur occasionally. Forget the name once you have secured a good specimen and introduce it to some water. This breed not only swims, it actually likes a dip – although be ready with a towel and give it a thorough drying afterwards.

Balinese

This is a long-haired version of the Siamese. It is exactly the same in body type and character, only the longer coat differing from the short-haired cat.

Tiffany

A fancy name for a fancy puss, but in fact the Tiffany is simply a Burmese with a longer coat. It has been produced by North American breeders.

Somali

This is the North American long-haired

version of the Abyssinian. Its longer coat can give it a rather wild appearance and poor specimens of the breed can suffer from excessive shyness, but otherwise the Somali shares all the virtues of the Abyssinian.

Maine Coon

A splendid cat with a splendid name, the Maine Coon is a long-established breed that probably developed from Domestic Shorthairs and Angora-type cats. It is a large and solidly built animal with a delicate-looking face (in this respect it resembles the Angora) and a long body, neck and tail. Its coat is not so long as the Persian and is relatively short on the shoulders, though becoming longer towards the tail and with heavy 'breeches' around the flanks and lower part of the body. There is a frontal ruff of hair and the ears are well tufted. A wide range of coat colours are accepted and the eyes may be green as well as gold or copper.

The Maine Coon is a friendly cat (perhaps just as well considering its size) and its coat needs less attention than other long-haired breeds. It is happiest with plenty of space outside, where it will prove a fearsomely effective mouser.

Cymric

This is a long-haired Manx. The breed originated in the United States, in the 1960s, as the result of a chance mutation. It gained recognition only in the 1970s and ownership is still confined to a rather limited number of enthusiasts.

Cat colours

That quick run-down of some of the breeds deals with the general types. There is a huge number of variations of colour and pattern, but every time you think there could not possibly be room for another, a breeder will produce a new one.

In fact, cats, like some cars, come in only three basic colours: black, red and white. The other colours are simply interminglings and the patterns made up of combinations of them. Their names are not straightforward to the uninitiated. The red, for example, is not red at all but a rich brownish-orange – though not the hot marmalade colour of some cats, which is not to the taste of fancy breeders. The dark-brown colour of the Seal Point Siamese is actually black, diluted by the same genetic combination that makes the Siamese points. Blue, which is really a shade of grey rather than a bright sky-blue, is another dilution of black (though blue eyes in cats really are azure blue). Cream is a weaker form of red, lilac a blue (grey) with a pinkish tinge, and there is a whole range of shades known as chocolate, milk chocolate, mink, and so on that are very much like what the names suggest. Tortoiseshell is a pattern made up of red, black and cream, and in America Calico is a similar combination with white, while Dilute Calico is a blue-cream mixture with white.

Despite a tradition that supposes gentleness in blues, colour has little to do with a cat's personality – though the development of colours in particular catteries may also have brought out characteristics in the strain. But white cats and tortoiseshell cats both have some genetic features that are colour-linked. White cats with blue eyes tend to be deaf – cats with orange eyes or with one of each, or cats which as kittens have a tiny patch of non-white fur, do not usually suffer, even though the kitten grows up to be a pure white cat. However, this cannot be predicted at birth since all kittens share blue eyes at first, then change to their adult colour later. Tortoiseshell cats are almost always female, and the rare males are sterile, so it is not possible to breed a tortoiseshell to a tortoiseshell. The tricolour pattern is sex-linked, so crosses have to be made to cats of a uniform black or red.

Some fur is patched with colour along the length of each hair; this is known as 'agouti' fur. It occurs in the Abyssinian and tabby cats. In other cats the fur is tipped with colour instead of being ticked along its length. This gives a sparkling effect to the fur when the tipping is very light, as in the Chinchilla (see page 42), which has white fur just tipped with black – but as the tipping extends down the hair the effect becomes darker, known, according to its length, as Cameo and Shaded. In the Smoke Cats, as they are called, the tipping is so strong that the cats appear solidly coloured until they move, when their white undercoat shines through – although Smoke Longhairs have a white ruff which gives the game away even when they are still.

Some coats, colours and patterns are genetically dominant over others. This has to be taken into account when planning breeding. Tabby, for example, is dominant over solid colours and can often be seen in kittens that later develop fully solid coats. But the genetics of inheritance in the cat are extremely complex and still not fully understood, and breeding cats is a labour of love, not of money. If you do not wish to breed you will hardly need to concern yourself, and should you wish to you will need to seek expert advice going far beyond the simple rules such as white is dominant over black, black over blue, solid colours over the Siamese point pattern and short fur over long fur. In any case, with the enormous range of cat varieties now available, why should you want to create yet another breed?

Cat shows

You can best see the enormous variety of cats by going to a show. Shows are usually arranged by cat clubs and associations according to very strict rules laid down by their governing body (such as the British Governing Council of the Cat Fancy). The pedigree classes will normally be open only to cats properly registered with that body, but local fêtes and festivals often have cat competitions that welcome all comers; and even the prestigious National Cat Club show held in London every year has classes for non-pedigree domestic moggies so that anyone can enter their pet.

With a large number of cats gathered together the risk of infectious disease is considerable, so it is essential that cats participating should be in good health. Competitors may be asked to produce certificates to prove that their cat has had recent vaccinations against the main diseases, and there may be an inspection by veterinarians at the show. Naturally, any cat that is found to carry parasites or to be otherwise unfit is likely to be barred from competition.

Individual regulations vary from show to show, as do the classes in which the cats compete. The system by which a cat collects a series of prize awards to become a champion, and the actual titles awarded, will also differ, particularly between British and American practices. The main difference to the visitor on crossing the Atlantic is that whereas American owners flamboyantly decorate their cat's pen with its previous awards and colourful drapes, the British cat is displayed in very simple surroundings with a plain white blanket, a litter tray and a bowl of water. After the judging has taken place any certificates or rosettes awarded may be displayed on the outside of the pen. If you see a decorated pen at a British show then it means that the cat is not competing, but is simply being shown because the owner wants to attract attention to a champion and the cattery.

The reason for the difference is quite simple. In North America the cats are taken from the pen to the judge – so the judges are not influenced by decorative display or records of former triumphs. In Britain the judges go to the pens, and they are allowed to know only the cat's catalogue number and the classes in which it has been entered.

Entering a show

Show exhibitors are enthusiasts, which means they will be delighted to talk to you about their cats and everything to do with them. They may even pass on a few tips if you are particularly charming. It is then a matter of deciding on the show and obtaining an entry form and the rules from the organizers.

Naturally you will want your cat to be in tip-top condition, and you will take particular care in grooming it in the weeks prior to the show itself. You will also need to get it used to show conditions. It is quite an ordeal for a cat to put up with, being bundled in a basket for the journey to and from, to sit patiently in a small pen for the best part of the day, to tolerate being handled by a couple of strangers – the judges – for every class in which it is entered, and to suffer the noise of the crowds milling around the show benches and staring at it all day long. The most even-tempered feline is likely to become thoroughly fed up. There is little you can do to avoid this, but you can at least try to accustom your cat to the impending mayhem by putting it into a similar pen under similar conditions for longer and longer spells until it learns to cope with the boredom of such restraint. Some breeders go so far as to play loud music near by in the hope that the cat will grow used to the din. Watch judges handling cats at shows and get your potential champion used to being subjected to these indignities – and used to being handled by strangers.

Even if an experienced cat does not help you to win prizes at least it will not end up in a state of panic from the shock of such public exposure. In fact it may well bask in all the attention that it gets. Could you cope with being pushed into a cage for half the world to stare at, and deprived of all home comforts, without becoming a screaming neurotic? Yet it is amazing how calm most show cats appear to be.

Of course, they may just be looking forward to a reward at the end of the day. Win or lose, they should be given some special treat when the ordeal is over – they will certainly have earned it! And after all your hard work so will you – but before you open the aqua vitae, you may well consider that the pleasure of being a cat owner is itself reward enough.

Index

Page numbers in italics indicate illustrations.

Picture credits

The publishers are grateful to the following for granting permission to reproduce copyright material: Page 41: Spectrum Colour Library. Pages 42, 43, 44, 93, 94 (below), 95 and 96: ZEFA Picture Library. Page 94 (above): Howard Loxton.